Why I Am a Christian

A clear, compelling account
of the basis of the author's belief

Inter-Varsity Press
36 Causton Street, London SW1P 4ST, England
Email: ivp@ivpbooks.com
Website: www.ivpbooks.com

First published 2003
Reprinted 2004, 2011, 2013
This edition 2021

British Library Cataloguing-in-Publication Data
A catalogue record for this book is available from the British Library.

ISBN: 978–1–78974–292–3

Set in Garamond
Typeset in Great Britain by Servis Filmsetting Ltd, Stockport, Cheshire
Printed and bound in Great Britain by 4edge Limited

Produced on paper from sustainable forests.

*Inter-Varsity Press publishes Christian books that are true to the Bible and that
communicate the gospel, develop discipleship and strengthen the church for its
mission in the world.*

*IVP originated within the Inter-Varsity Fellowship, now the Universities and
Colleges Christian Fellowship, a student movement connecting Christian Unions
in universities and colleges throughout Great Britain, and a member movement
of the International Fellowship of Evangelical Students. Website: www.uccf.org.
uk. That historic association is maintained, and all senior IVP staff and committee
members subscribe to the UCCF Basis of Faith.*

JOHN
STOTT
100

Dedicated
to the memory of
Canon Miles Thomson
Rector of St Nicholas' Church, Sevenoaks, Kent,
1987–2000,
and a good soldier of Jesus Christ

CONTENTS

PREFACE

It was on 6 March 1927 that Bertrand Russell gave a public address in Battersea Town Hall, South London, entitled 'Why I am *not* a Christian'. It made quite a sensation at the time, partly because of the well-known eloquence of the speaker, and partly because of his sheer outspokenness. Thirty years later his speech was published in a collection of his essays. It was chapter 1, and it gave its title to the whole book.[1]

In his preface Bertrand Russell wrote: 'I think all the great religions of the world ... both untrue and harmful' (p. xi). Although he had some difficulty in defining the kind of 'Christian' he declared he was not, he was able to demolish to his satisfaction the traditional arguments for the existence of God.

In writing this short book entitled *Why I AM a Christian*, I am not presuming to rebut Earl Russell's arguments point by point, for I acknowledge his brilliance as mathematician-philosopher, Nobel Prize-winner for literature and champion of logic and liberty. But I also acknowledge that there is a case to be made for Christianity that Bertrand Russell did not make or even consider.

I am grateful to Richard Bewes, Rector of All Souls Church, Langham Place, London, for inviting me in 1986 to preach four sermons on this topic. Among those who later listened to the tapes was my friend, the late Miles Thomson, Rector of St Nicholas' Church, Sevenoaks. He kept urging me to write up those four sermons into a book and to add a chapter or two. Such a book, he wrote, 'would provide a fuller introduction than any of the current smaller booklets. At the same time, it would not be too heavy or too big for a genuine enquirer who wants to think through the implications of becoming a Christian.'

So, having yielded to Miles Thomson's importunity, I dedicate this modest piece to his memory. *Milès* is Latin for 'soldier', and that is what Miles was, a good soldier of Jesus Christ.

I thank my friends Paul Weston and Roger Simpson for reading the typescript of this book. They made a number of suggestions, most of which I have adopted. I also thank Stephanie Heald, IVP's Senior Commissioning Editor, for her attention to detail. In addition, I am extremely grateful to Frances Whitehead, my secretary, for producing yet one more flawless text.

I confess that I have freely borrowed for this text from what I have written in other contexts, especially in *The Contemporary Christian* (1992).[2] But I have been assured, by friends and publishers alike, that this overlap does not matter, since my personal statement or story in this book can stand on its own feet.

John Stott
New Year 2003

For the Son of Man came to seek and to save what was lost.

LUKE 19:10

Chapter 1

THE HOUND OF HEAVEN

Rapid travel and the electronic media have made us all aware (as never before) of the multiplicity of religions in the world. So how on earth can we decide between them? There is a Babel of voices competing for our attention. To which are we going to listen? We are presented with a veritable religious *smorgasbord*. So which dish are we going to choose? In any case, do not all religions lead to God?

It is against this pluralistic background that I want to answer the question: Why am I a Christian? Some readers will expect me to answer like this: 'I'm a Christian because I happen to have been born in a largely Christian country. My parents were nominally Christian, I went to a school with a Christian foundation and I received a basically Christian education.' In other words it was the circumstances of my birth, parentage and upbringing that have determined the fact that I am a Christian. And that is, of course, perfectly true. But it is only a part of the truth. For I could have repudiated my Christian inheritance. Many people do. And there are many others who become Christians who have not had a Christian upbringing. So that is not the complete answer.

Others may expect me to reply something like this. 'On 13 February 1938, when I was a youth of nearly seventeen, I made a decision for Christ. I heard a clergyman preach on Pilate's question, "What shall I do with Jesus, who is called Christ?" Until that moment I didn't know I had to do anything with Jesus, who is called Christ. But in answer to my questions, the preacher unfolded the steps to Christ. In particular, he pointed me in the New Testament to Revelation 3:20, in which Jesus says: "Here I am! I stand at the door and knock. If anyone hears my voice and opens the door, I will come in and eat with him, and he with me." So that night, by my bedside, I opened the door of my personality to Christ, inviting him to come in as my Saviour and Lord.'

That also is true, but it constitutes only one side of the truth.

The most significant factor lies elsewhere, and it is on this that I intend to concentrate in this first chapter. Why I am a Christian is due ultimately neither to the influence of my parents and teachers, nor to my own personal decision for Christ, but to 'the Hound of Heaven'. That is, it is due to Jesus Christ himself, who pursued me relentlessly even when I was running away from him in order to go my own way. And if it were not for the gracious pursuit of the Hound of Heaven I would today be on the scrap-heap of wasted and discarded lives.

FRANCIS THOMPSON

'The Hound of Heaven.' It is a striking expression invented by Francis Thompson, whose story has been told, and his poem expounded, by R. Moffat Gautrey in his book *This Tremendous Lover*.[1]

Francis Thompson spent a lonely and loveless childhood, and failed successively in his attempts to become a Roman Catholic priest, a doctor (like his father) and a soldier. He ended up lost in London until a Christian couple recognized his poetic genius and rescued him. Throughout these years he was conscious of both pursuing and being pursued, and expressed it most eloquently in his poem 'the Hound of Heaven'. Here is its beginning:

> I fled Him, down the nights and down the days;
>   I fled Him, down the arches of the years;
> I fled Him, down the labyrinthine ways
>   Of my own mind; and in the midst of tears
> I hid from Him, and under running laughter.
>   Up vistaed hopes I sped;
>   And shot, precipitated,
> Adown Titanic glooms of chasmèd fears,
>   From those strong Feet that followed, followed after.
>   But with unhurrying chase,

> And unperturbèd pace,
> Deliberate speed, majestic instancy,
>   They beat – and a Voice beat
>   More instant than the Feet –
> 'All things betray thee, who betrayest Me.'[2]

At first R. M. Gautrey was offended by the poem's title 'The Hound of Heaven'. Is it appropriate, he asked himself, to liken God to a hound? But he came to see that there are good hounds as well as bad hounds, and that specially admirable are collies, which range the Scottish Highlands in search of lost sheep. He also saw that the theme of searching sheepdogs (or, more accurately, of searching shepherds) occurs in both the Old and the New Testament. Thus, the last verse of Psalm 23 reads:

> Surely goodness and love will follow me
>   all the days of my life,
> and I will dwell in the house of the LORD for ever.

Gautrey points out that the Hebrew word here translated by the mild verb 'follow' should be rendered more forcefully; for instance, 'goodness and mercy have hunted me, haunted me, dogged my steps all the days of my life'.[3] 'It is a pursuit, patient but purposeful, affectionate but relentless.'[4]

Then Jesus himself took up the metaphor of the shepherd:

> Then Jesus told them this parable: 'Suppose one of you has a

hundred sheep and loses one of them. Does he not leave the ninety-nine in the open country and go after the lost sheep until he finds it? And when he finds it, he joyfully puts it on his shoulders and goes home. Then he calls his friends and neighbours together and says, "Rejoice with me; I have found my lost sheep." I tell you that in the same way there will be more rejoicing in heaven over one sinner who repents than over ninety-nine righteous persons who do not need to repent.' (Luke 15:3–7).

Gautrey sees the poem as divided into five stanzas. The first he calls the 'Soul's Flight', for the poet sees himself as a fugitive from the demands of discipleship. The second is the 'Soul's Quest', in which the soul seeks satisfaction everywhere, but cannot find it. The third stanza he entitles the 'Soul's Impasse', since he has discovered that life without God is meaningless. Fourthly, in the 'Soul's Arrest', he finally surrenders to the love of Christ. Christ speaks to him:

'Alack, thou knowest not
How little worthy of any love thou art!
Whom wilt thou find to love ignoble thee,
    Save Me, save only Me?'[5]

In every stanza we hear that footfall of 'this tremendous lover', until finally the hunt is over:

'All which I took from thee I did but take,
    Not for thy harms,   •

But just that thou might'st seek it in My arms ...
    Rise, clasp My hand, and come!'[6]

Francis Thompson was expressing what is true of every Christian; it has certainly been true in my life. If we love Christ, it is because he loved us first (1 John 4:19). If we are Christians at all, it is not because we have decided for Christ, but because Christ has decided for us. It is because of the pursuit of 'this tremendous lover'.

If we love Christ, it is because he loved us first.

For evidence that the initiative is his, I invite you to take with me a fresh look at the conversion of Saul of Tarsus, and then at three Christian biographies. Then I shall come back briefly to us, to me, who am writing to you, and to you who are reading.

SAUL OF TARSUS

First, Saul of Tarsus. His conversion is the most celebrated in the whole history of the Christian church. Some people, however, are troubled by it. 'I've had no sudden Damascus-road experience,' they say. But consider. Saul's conversion was not sudden. Does that surprise you? Of course, it is true that suddenly a light flashed from heaven, and suddenly he fell to the ground and Jesus spoke to him. But that suddenness of the intervention of Jesus was not by any means the first time that Jesus had spoken to him. On the contrary, it was the climax of a long process. How do we know that? Let me refer you to Acts 26:14: 'We all fell to the ground, and I heard a voice saying to me in Aramaic, "Saul, Saul, why do you persecute me? It is hard for you to kick against the goads."'

The Greek word *kentron* could be translated 'spur', 'whip' or 'goad'. Quite frequently in classical Greek, from Aeschylus onwards, it was used in a metaphorical sense. Similarly, in the book of Proverbs we read:

A whip for the horse, a halter for the donkey,
    and a rod for the backs of fools!' (26:3).

In speaking to Saul, Jesus was likening himself either to a farmer goading a recalcitrant bullock or to a horse-trainer breaking in a rather rumbustious young colt. The implication is clear. Jesus was pursuing, prodding and pricking Saul. But Saul was resisting the pressure, and it was hard, it was painful, even futile, for him to kick against the goads.

This raises the natural question: what were the goads with which Jesus Christ was pricking Saul of Tarsus? Although we're not told specifically, we can piece together the evidence from the book of Acts and from autobiographical flashes in Paul's later letters.

1. *Jesus was goading Saul in his mind.* Saul had been educated in Jerusalem under Gamaliel, probably the most celebrated Jewish teacher throughout the whole of the first

century AD. So, theologically, Saul was well versed in Judaism, and morally, he was zealous for the law. With his conscious mind in those days, he was convinced that Jesus of Nazareth was not the Messiah. To him it was inconceivable that the Jewish Messiah could be rejected by his own people and then die, apparently under the curse of God, since it was written in the law that 'anyone who is hung on a tree is under God's curse' (Deuteronomy 21:23). No, no. Jesus must be an impostor. So Saul saw it as his plain duty to oppose Jesus of Nazareth and to persecute his followers. That was the conviction of his conscious mind. Subconsciously, however, his mind was full of doubts because of the rumours that were circulating about Jesus: the beauty and authority of his teaching; the meekness and gentleness of his character; his compassionate service of the poor; his mighty works of healing, and especially the persistent rumour that his death had not been the end of him, for people were claiming to have seen him, touched him and talked with him after his death. His mind was in turmoil.

2. *Jesus was goading Saul in his memory.* He had evidently been present at the trial before the Sanhedrin of a Christian leader named Stephen, whom Luke described as 'a man full of faith and of the Holy Spirit' (Acts 6:5). This, then, was not rumour or hearsay. For Saul had seen with his own eyes Stephen's face shining like the face of an angel (Acts 6:15). He had heard with his own ears Stephen's defence, at the end of which Stephen had claimed to see the glory of God and 'the Son of Man standing at the right

hand of God' (Acts 7:55–56). Then, when they drove Stephen out of town and stoned him to death, they laid their clothes at the feet of Saul. Luke continues his description: 'While they were stoning him, Stephen prayed, "Lord Jesus, receive my spirit." Then he fell on his knees and cried out, "Lord, do not hold this sin against them." When he had said this, he fell asleep' (Acts 7:59–60).

Saul must have said to himself, 'There's something inexplicable about these Christians. They are convinced that Jesus of Nazareth is the Messiah and they have the courage of their convictions; they're prepared to die for them. Moreover, they refuse to retaliate against their enemies, but pray for them instead.' Jesus was goading Saul's memory. He couldn't get Stephen out of his mind.

3. *Jesus was goading Saul in his conscience.* Saul was an extremely righteous man, as all Pharisees were. He lived an unblemished life and he had an unblemished reputation. As he wrote in one of his later letters, as touching the righteousness of the law he was blameless (Philippians 3:6). And yet the blameless righteousness that he claimed to possess was a purely external conformity to the requirements of the law. Outwardly he had obeyed the precepts and the prohibitions of the law. Inwardly, however, in his conscience, he knew that he was sinful. He could have said, as C. S. Lewis was to write years later: 'For the first time I examined myself with a seriously practical purpose. And there I found what appalled me; a zoo of lusts, a bedlam of ambitions, a nursery of fears, a harem of fondled hatreds. My name was legion.'[7]

In Saul's case it was the last of the Ten Commandments that convicted him. He could manage the first nine reasonably well because they had to do only with his words and deeds. But the tenth prohibited covetousness. And covetousness is neither a deed nor a word but a desire, an insatiable lust. And so, when he came across that commandment he wrote in the very dramatic imagery of Romans 7 that it slew him.

Saul believed in God, but he didn't know him.

I would not have known what sin was except through the law. For I would not have known what coveting really was if the law had not said, 'Do not covet.' But sin ... produced in me every kind of covetous desire ... Once I was alive apart from law; but when the commandment came, sin sprang to life and I died (Romans 7:7–9).

4. *Jesus was goading Saul in his spirit.* I use this word in reference to that part of our human make-up which is aware of the transcendent reality of God. As a Jew Saul had believed in God, of course, from his childhood. He'd sought to serve God from his youth with a clear conscience, and yet he knew that he was separated from the very God he believed in. He believed in him, but he didn't know him. He was alienated from him. He said so in the text I have just quoted: 'when the commandment came

... I died.' To use his later language, he was 'dead in ... transgressions and sins' (Ephesians 2:1), estranged from God the life-giver.

These, I suggest, were the goads with which Jesus Christ was pricking Saul of Tarsus, and which Saul was kicking against to his own hurt. He pricked him in his mind (filling it with doubts as to whether Jesus was an impostor or true). He pricked him in his memory (reminding him of Stephen's face, words, dignity and death). He pricked him in his conscience (convicting him of evil desires). And he pricked him in his spirit, in that vast, empty vacuum of alienation. In these ways for years Jesus had been pricking and prodding Saul, hurting him only in order to heal him. And the very fanaticism with which Saul was persecuting Christ by persecuting the church betrayed his inner uneasiness. So when Jesus appeared to him on the Damascus road, it was the sudden climax of a gradual process. Saul finally surrendered to the one whom he had long been fighting and fleeing.

AUGUSTINE

I move on now to some Christian biographies, and I begin with that great early-church father, Augustine of Hippo. He was born in North Africa (in what we now call Algeria) in the middle of the fourth century. Already in his teens he was leading a dissolute, even promiscuous, life, enslaved by his passions. He wrote in his *Confessions*:

> Clouds of muddy carnal concupiscence filled the air. The bubbling impulses of puberty befogged and obscured my heart so

that it could not see the difference between love's serenity and lust's darkness. Confusion of the two things boiled within me. It seized hold of my youthful weakness sweeping me through the precipitous rocks of desire to submerge me in a whirlpool of vice.[8]

Even while half-drowned in sin, Augustine also plunged into study, and his studies took him first to Carthage, and then to Rome and to Milan. A great tug of war was going on in his mind between Christianity (which at this time he rejected) and Manicheism (which he had embraced). In this turmoil of moral shame and intellectual confusion he found himself in utter misery. Yet, through his inner restlessness of mind and conscience, as also through the prayers and tears of his saintly mother Monica, and through the kindly admonitions of Bishop Ambrose of Milan, Jesus Christ was surely pursuing him.

As with Saul of Tarsus, so with Augustine of Hippo, the climax came suddenly. He went out into the garden attached to his lodgings, accompanied by his friend Alypius. He threw himself down under a tree and let his tears flow freely, as he cried out, 'How long, O Lord?'

As I was saying this and weeping in the bitter agony of my heart, suddenly I heard a voice from the nearby house chanting as if it might be a boy or a girl (I do not know which), saying and repeating over and over again, 'pick up and read, pick up and read ...' I checked the flood of tears and stood up. I interpreted it solely as a divine command to me to open the book and read the first chapter I might find ... So I hurried back to the place where Alypius was sitting. There I had put down the book of the apostle when I got up. I seized it, opened it and in silence read the first passage on which my eyes lit: 'Not in riots and drunken parties, not in eroticism and indecencies, not in strife and rivalry, but put on the Lord Jesus Christ and make no provision for the flesh in its lusts' (Romans 13:13–14).

I neither wished nor needed to read further. At once, with the last words of this sentence, it was as if a light of relief from all anxiety flooded into my heart. All the shadows of doubt were dispelled.[9]

Augustine attributed his experience to the sheer grace, that is, the free and unmerited favour, of God. He claimed that God had quickened all five of his spiritual senses – hearing, sight, smell, taste and touch:

You called and cried out loud and shattered my deafness. You were radiant and resplendent, you put to flight my blindness. You were fragrant, and I drew in my breath and now pant after you. I tasted you, and I feel but hunger and thirst for you. You touched me, and I am set on fire to attain the peace which is yours.[10]

But Paul belonged to the first century, and Augustine to the fourth and fifth. It is time to move into our own era and see that the Hound of Heaven is still chasing people today.

MALCOLM MUGGERIDGE
Malcolm Muggeridge was a well-known figure in the second half of the twentieth century – literateur, television

personality and Christian spokesman. He described in the first part of his autobiography how, soon after graduating from Cambridge, he spent time in a remote part of South India. He wrote:

> I had a notion that somehow, besides questing, I was being pursued. Footsteps padding behind me; a following shadow, a Hound of Heaven, so near that I could feel the warm breath on my neck ... I was also in flight. Chasing and being chased; the pursuing and the pursuit, the quest and the flight, merging at last into one single immanence or luminosity.[11]

Muggeridge made his experience the more dramatic by expressing it in a direct second-person encounter:

> Yes, You were there, I know ... How ever far and fast I've run, still over my shoulder I'd catch a glimpse of You on the horizon, and then run faster and farther than ever, thinking triumphantly: Now I have escaped. But no, there You were, coming after me ... One shivers as the divine beast of prey gets ready for the final spring ... There is no escape.[12]

C. S. LEWIS
But nobody has expressed this sense of the divine pursuit more eloquently than C. S. Lewis (1898–1963), whose honest account I have already referred to. Lewis was an Oxford and Cambridge scholar, literary critic, children's fiction-writer and Christian apologist.

For some time before his conversion Lewis was aware that God was after him. In his autobiographical sketch

Surprised by Joy[13] he piles up metaphors to illustrate it. First, God was 'the great Angler', playing his fish, 'and I never dreamed that the hook was in my tongue'.[14] Next, he likened God to a cat chasing a mouse. 'Amiable agnostics will talk cheerfully about "man's search for God". To me … they might as well have talked about the mouse's search for the cat.'[15] Thirdly, he likened God to a pack of hounds. 'The fox had been dislodged from the Hegelian Wood and was now running in the open … bedraggled and weary, hounds barely a field behind. And nearly everyone now (one way or another) in the pack …'[16] Finally, God was the Divine Chessplayer, gradually manoeuvring him into an impossible position. 'All over the board my pieces were in the most disadvantageous positions. Soon I could no longer cherish even the illusion that the initiative lay with me. My Adversary began to make His final moves.'[17] So Lewis entitled his penultimate chapter 'Checkmate'.[18]

God was the Divine Chessplayer, gradually manoevring him into an impossible position.

Lewis's actual moment of surrender to Christ in Oxford he described in memorable words:

You must picture me alone in that room at Magdalen, night after night, feeling, whenever my mind lifted even for a second from my work, the steady, unrelenting approach of Him whom I so earnestly desired not to meet. That which I greatly feared had at last come upon me. In the Trinity Term of 1929 I gave in, and admitted that God was God, and knelt and prayed: perhaps, that night, the most dejected and reluctant convert in all England. I did not then see what is now the most shining and obvious thing; the Divine humility which will accept a convert even on such terms. The Prodigal Son at least walked home on his own feet. But who can duly adore that Love which will open the high gates to a prodigal who is brought in kicking, struggling, resentful, and darting his eyes in every direction for a chance of escape? ... The hardness of God is kinder than the softness of men, and His compulsion is our liberation.[19]

We must not suppose, however, that the Hound of Heaven pursues only VIPs like Saul of Tarsus, Augustine of Hippo, Malcolm Muggeridge and C. S. Lewis. Multitudes of ordinary people have testified down the Christian centuries to the same sense of Christ knocking at their door or pricking them with his goads or pursuing them.

I think I can do so myself. Indeed, because I am writing on *Why I Am a Christian*, I cannot avoid being personal and telling my story. Looking back over a long life, I have often asked myself what it was that brought me to Christ. As I have said already, it was neither my parental upbringing nor my own independent choice; it was Christ himself knocking at my door, drawing attention to his presence outside.

He did this in two major ways. The first was my sense of estrangement from God. I was no atheist. I believed in the existence of God – someone or something somewhere, the ultimate reality behind and beyond all phenomena. But I could not find him. I used to visit a dark little chapel in the school I was attending, in order to read religious books and recite prayers. All to no avail. God was remote and aloof; I was unable to penetrate the fog that seemed to envelop him.

The second way in which I heard Christ knocking at my door was through my sense of defeat. With the vibrant idealism of youth I had a heroic picture of the sort of person I wanted to be – kind, unselfish and public-spirited. But I had an equally clear picture of who I was – malicious, self-centred and proud. The two pictures did not coincide. I was high-idealled but weak-willed.

Did I open the door, or did he?

Yet through my sense of alienation and failure the Stranger at the door kept knocking, until the preacher I mentioned at the beginning of this chapter threw light on my dilemma. He spoke to me of the death and resurrection of Jesus Christ. He explained that Christ had died to turn my estrangement into reconciliation, and had been raised from the dead to turn my defeat into victory. The correspondence between my subjective need and Christ's objective offer seemed too close to be a coincidence. Christ's knocking became louder and more insistent. Did I open the door, or did he? Truly I did, but only because by his persistent knocking he had made it possible, even inevitable.

I have told you my story; I wonder about yours. Jesus assures us in his parables that, whether or not we are consciously seeking God, he is assuredly seeking us. He is like a woman who sweeps her house in search of a lost coin; like a shepherd who risks the dangers of the desert in search of only one lost sheep; and like a father who misses his wayward son and allows him to taste the bitterness of his folly, but is ready at any moment to run to meet him and welcome him home.

I am persuaded that at some point in our lives we have felt the pricking and heard the knocking of Jesus Christ, even though we may not have recognized what it was. For there are many different ways in which he seeks us, pursues us and warns us when we are on the wrong road and heading in the wrong direction.

Sometimes it is through a sense of shame and guilt, as we remember something we have thought, said or done and are horrified by the depths of depravity to which we are capable of sinking.

Or it may be the deep, dark pit of depression, or the void of existential despair, in which nothing makes sense and everything is absurd. Or it may be the fear of death and of the possibility of judgment after death.

Alternatively and positively, we may on occasion be overwhelmed with wonder at the delicate balances of nature, or by something stunningly beautiful to the ear, the eye or the touch. Or again we may experience either the ecstasy of undeserved love or the acute pain of un-requited love, because we know instinctively that love is the greatest thing in the world. It is in such moments as these that Jesus Christ draws near to us and uses his hand to knock or to goad.

If we become aware of the relentless pursuit of Christ, and give up trying to escape from him, and surrender to the embrace of 'this tremendous lover', there will be no room for boasting in what we have done, but only for profound thanksgiving for his grace and mercy, and for the firm resolve to spend time and eternity in his loving service.

The Spirit of the Lord is on me,

because he has anointed me

to preach good news to the poor.

He has sent me to proclaim freedom for the prisoners

and recovery of sight for the blind,

to release the oppressed,

to proclaim the year of the Lord's favour.

LUKE 4:18,19

Chapter 2

THE CLAIMS OF JESUS

My first answer to the question 'Why am I a Christian?' has been to refer to the Hound of Heaven, who pursued, pricked and prodded me until I surrendered to him. My second answer is, 'Because I am convinced that Christianity is true, or better, that the claims of Jesus are true.'

In our tolerant, pluralistic society, whenever someone becomes a Christian, the usual patronizing comment is: 'How nice! I'm sure it will be a great help to you. We need the comfort of religion in our hard and threatening times.'

Well, I don't for a moment deny that Jesus Christ is an enormous help and comfort to his followers. But he also poses a radical challenge. So the second reason why I am a Christian is not that it is nice but that it is true.

Our postmodern culture, in reaction to the self-confidence of modernity, has lost all sense of assurance and affirms that there is no such thing as objective or universal truth. All our understanding is held to be culturally conditioned, is relative, and everybody has his or her own truth. Christians have a different conviction, however, namely that there is such a thing as objective truth.

A good example of this claim is the example of the apostle Paul during one of his trials (Acts 26). Standing before King Agrippa, and being given liberty to speak, Paul told the story of his Jewish upbringing, his persecution of the church, his dramatic conversion and his commissioning as the apostle to the Gentiles. He proclaimed that the Messiah had to suffer and to be the first person to rise from the dead.

> *Not that it is nice but that it is true.*

At this point Festus, procurator of the Roman province of Judea, interrupted Paul's defence and shouted, 'You are out of your mind, Paul! Your great learning is driving you insane.'

'I am not insane, most excellent Festus', Paul responded calmly. 'What I am saying is true and reasonable' (see verses 24–25). Indeed, it is reasonable precisely because it is true. I could say the same.

Let's be clear, to begin with, that the claims of Christianity are in essence the claims of Christ. I have no particular wish to defend 'Christianity' as a system or 'the church' as an institution. The history of the church has been a bitter-sweet story, combining deeds of heroism with deeds of shame. But we are not ashamed of Jesus Christ, who is the centre and core of Christianity.

Indeed, there are many people who are critical of the church, yet who at the same time retain a sneaking admiration for Jesus. In fact, I have never yet met anybody, nor do I expect to, who does not have a high regard for Jesus Christ. Jesus appeals to twenty-first-century people like us. He was a fearless critic of the establishment. He championed the cause of the poor and needy. He made friends with the drop-

> *Jesus Christ is the centre and core of Christianity.*

outs of society. He had compassion on the very people whom others despised and rejected. And although he was fiercely and unjustly attacked, he never retaliated. He told his disciples that they must love their enemies, and he practised what he preached. There is a great deal about Jesus to admire.

Without doubt the most noteworthy feature of the teaching of Jesus was its quite extraordinary self-centredness. He was, in fact, constantly talking about himself. True, he spoke much about the kingdom of God, but then added that he had come to inaugurate it. He also spoke about the fatherhood of God, but added that he was the Father's 'Son'.

In the great 'I am' statements, which John records in his Gospel, Jesus claimed to be 'the bread of life', 'the light of the world', 'the way, the truth and the life' and 'the resurrection and the life'. But elsewhere too he put himself forward as the object of people's faith. 'Come to me' and 'Follow me', he kept saying, promising that if they did come, their burdens would be lifted and their thirst quenched (e.g. Matthew 11:28; John 7:37). More dramatic still were his references to love. He knew and quoted the supreme Old Testament commandment to put God first and love him with all our being. But now he asked his followers to give *him* their first love, adding that if they loved anybody – even their closest relatives – more than they loved him, they were not worthy of him (e.g. Matthew 10:37–39).

This prominence of the personal pronoun ('I – I – I – me – me – me') is very disturbing, especially in one who declared humility to be the pre-eminent virtue. It also sets Jesus apart from all the other religious leaders of the world. They effaced themselves, pointing away from themselves to the truth they taught; he advanced himself, offering himself to his disciples as the object of their faith, love and obedience. There is no doubt, then, that Jesus believed he was unique, and it is this self-consciousness of Jesus which we need to investigate further. There were three main strands of it, three relationships that he claimed – firstly to the Old Testament Scriptures, secondly to the one he called his Father, and thirdly to the rest of humankind, including ourselves.

FULFILMENT

First, in relation to Old Testament Scripture, Jesus claimed to be its fulfilment.

This sense of fulfilment was an essential ingredient of his self-consciousness from the beginning to the end of his public ministry. His first recorded word according to the Greek of Mark's Gospel was *peplērōtai*, 'fulfilled'. He proclaimed: 'The time has come [literally, 'has been fulfilled'] ... The kingdom of God is near. Repent and believe the good news!'

There is no doubt that Jesus believed he was unique.

(Mark 1:15). That is, the kingdom or rule of God, long promised in the Old Testament, had at last arrived; he himself had come to usher it in. In consequence, if people would but humble themselves, repent and believe in him, they could 'enter' or 'inherit' the kingdom there and then.

Consider next the dramatic incident recorded in Luke 4:14–21, which took place in his home village of Nazareth on a certain Sabbath day. Jesus attended the synagogue service, as was his custom. He was given the scroll of the

prophet Isaiah from which to read, and the set lesson was
from our chapter 61:

> 'The Spirit of the Lord is on me,
>   because he has anointed me
>   to preach good news to the poor.
> He has sent me to proclaim freedom for the prisoners
>   and recovery of sight for the blind,
> to release the oppressed,
>   to proclaim the year of the Lord's favour'
> (Luke 4:18–19; cf. Isaiah 61:1–2).

Having finished the reading, Jesus rolled up the Isaiah
scroll, returned it to the synagogue attendant and sat
down, ready, as a visiting rabbi, to expound the reading.
And as the eyes of the congregation were fastened on him,
he astonished them by saying: 'Today this scripture is fulfilled (*peplērōtai* again) in your hearing' (Luke 4:21). In
other words, 'If you want to know to whom the prophet
was referring, he was writing about me.' It was an extraordinary claim to be the fulfilment of Scripture.

So Jesus continued to affirm that 'the Scriptures ...
testify about me' (John 5:39) and that 'Abraham rejoiced
at the thought of seeing my day' (John 8:56). And after his
resurrection 'he explained to them what was said in all the
Scriptures concerning himself', adding, 'Everything must
be fulfilled that is written about me in the Law of Moses,
the Prophets and the Psalms' (Luke 24:27, 44).

In particular, Jesus saw himself in two Old Testament
figures. The first was 'the son of man', a human person in

Daniel's vision, who 'was given authority, glory and sovereign power', so that 'all people, nations and men of every language worshipped him' and his dominion would be 'an everlasting dominion that will not pass away' (Daniel 7:13–14).

But Jesus also saw himself as Isaiah's 'suffering servant', who 'was despised and rejected by men' and 'bore the sin of many' (Isaiah 53:3, 12). Thus 'son of man' in Daniel 7 was a title of honour, while 'suffering servant' in Isaiah 53 was a title of shame. Then Jesus did what nobody had ever done before him. He fused the two images by saying that the Son of Man must suffer many things (Mark 8:31). He insisted that it was only through suffering and death that he would enter into his glory.

> *Their eyes were actually seeing, and their ears actually hearing, what the Old Testament prophets had longed to hear and see.*

One day, as recorded by Matthew and Luke, Jesus made his strongest and clearest statement: 'Blessed are your eyes because they see, and your ears because they hear. For I tell you the truth, many prophets and righteous men longed to see what you see but did not see it, and to hear what you hear but did not hear it' (Matthew 13:16–17; cf. Luke 10:23–24). In other words, their eyes were actually seeing, and their ears actually hearing, what the Old Testament prophets had longed to hear and see for themselves, but did not. The prophets lived in the time of anticipation, the disciples in the days of fulfilment.

It is a highly significant claim. For many people are prepared to regard Jesus as a prophet, including the whole world of Islam. But Jesus neither thought nor spoke of himself in those terms. On the contrary. Instead of being one more prophet in the long succession of the centuries – even the final prophet – Jesus claimed rather to be the fulfilment of all prophecy. All the varied prophetic streams of the Old Testament converged on him. It was in and with his coming that the new age had dawned and the kingdom of God had at last arrived.

INTIMACY

Secondly, in relation to God, whom he called 'Father', Jesus claimed the unique relationship of 'Son'.

I deliberately add the adjective 'unique', because the use of the term or title 'son of God' is not by itself definitive. The expression is used in Scripture in a wide variety of ways. Angels are occasionally called 'sons of God' (e.g. Job 1:6; 2:1). So was Adam (Luke 3:38). So were Solomon (2 Samuel 7:14) and Israel as a whole (Exodus 4:22; Hosea 11:1). In fact, the term came to be applied to all the anointed kings of Judah, and especially to the coming Davidic king, the Messiah (e.g. Psalm 2:7).

So the title by itself is not conclusive. After all, we who seek to follow Jesus today are permitted to call ourselves the sons and daughters of God. Yet the way in which Jesus used the term was distinctive. To begin with, he gave it the definite article, calling God 'the Father', and himself 'the Son', in fact the Father's unique Son (Matthew 11:27), in an absolute and unqualified way. We may claim to be 'a' son or 'a' daughter of God, but we would not dream of calling ourselves 'the' daughter or 'the' son. Yet Jesus did, and thereby implied that there existed between himself and the Father a unique reciprocal relationship, which enabled him to say, 'no-one knows the Son except the Father, and no-one knows the Father except the Son' (Matthew 11:27). And he expressed this unique intimacy of relationship by addressing God as 'Abba', 'my Father'.

The late Professor Joachim Jeremias of Göttingen (1900–82) wrote about the significance of this:

> To date nobody has produced one single instance in Palestinian Judaism where God is addressed as 'my Father' by an individual person … But Jesus did just this … The most remarkable thing is that when Jesus addressed God as his Father in prayer he used the Aramaic word 'Abba' … Nowhere in the literature and the prayers of ancient Judaism – an immense treasure all too little explored – is this invocation of God as *Abba* to be found … Jesus on the other hand always used it when he prayed … To a Jewish mind it would have been irreverent and therefore unthinkable to call God by this familiar word. It was something new, something unique and unheard of, that Jesus dared to take this step and to speak with God as a child speaks with his father, simply, intimately, securely … *Abba* as an address to God is *ipsissima vox* [the very voice itself], an authentic and original utterance of Jesus …[1]

We do not of course fully understand the self-consciousness of Jesus. Nor do we know how he came to experience the fatherhood of God. But we do know that, already at the tender age of twelve, he thought of God as his Father and was able to ask, 'Didn't you know I had to be in my Father's house?' (Luke 2:49). We also know that his intimate relationship with the Father continued throughout his life, even through his sufferings (except for that horrendous moment of God-forsakenness on the cross), until his final words when he died, which were, 'Father, into your hands I commit my spirit' (Luke 23:46).

AUTHORITY

Thirdly, in relation to human beings Jesus claimed the authority to be their saviour and their judge.

One of the most extraordinary things Jesus did in his teaching (and did it so unobtrusively that many people read the Gospels without even noticing it) was to set himself apart from everybody else. For example, by claiming to be the good shepherd who went out into the desert to seek his lost sheep, he was implying that the world was lost, that he wasn't, and that he could seek and save it.

In other words, he put himself in a moral category in which he was alone. Everybody else was in darkness; he was the light of the world. Everybody else was hungry; he was the bread of life. Everybody else was thirsty; he could quench their thirst. Everybody else was sinful; he could forgive their sins. Indeed, on two separate occasions he did so, and both times observers were scandalized. They asked, 'Why does this fellow talk like that? He's blas-pheming! Who can forgive sins but God alone?' (Mark 2:5–7; cf. Luke 7:48–49).

If Jesus claimed authority to forgive the penitent, he also claimed authority to judge the impenitent. Several of his parables implied that he expected to return at the end of history. On that day, he said, he would sit on his glori-ous throne. All nations would stand before him, and he would separate them from one another as a shepherd separates his sheep from his goats. In other words, he would settle their eternal destiny. Thus he made himself the central figure on the day of judgment.

Some declared that he must be mad. Others left everything, rose up and followed him.

These are breathtaking claims. Jesus was by trade a carpenter. Nazareth was an obscure village on the edge of the Roman Empire. Nobody outside Palestine would even have heard of Nazareth. Yet here he is, claiming to be the saviour and the judge of all humankind.

People were amazed by his authority. They felt awe and wonder in his presence. Some declared that he must be mad. Others left everything, rose up and followed him.

Here, then, are the three main relationships that Jesus claimed. In relation to the Old Testament Scriptures, he

was their fulfilment. In relation to God the Father, he
enjoyed the unique intimacy of sonship. In relation to
human beings, he claimed authority to be their saviour
and their judge. Three words encapsulate his claims – fulfilment, intimacy and authority. He claimed to be the
Christ of Scripture, the Son of God and the saviour and
judge of the world.

'My reading of the Gospels', wrote Hugh Martin, a
New Testament scholar, 'after the closest scrutiny and
making all allowances, is that Jesus never ceased in word
and act to claim lordship over the hearts and lives of men.
We may regret that, we may resent it, but the fact cannot
be denied. The evidence in all our documents is incontro-
vertible.'[2]

What, then, do we make of his claims? One thing we
cannot do (though many people try to) is ignore them. If
we sweep them under the carpet, they have the disconcert-
ing habit of popping out again. They are woven into the
texture of the Gospels; we cannot pretend they are not
there. We cannot dress Jesus up as a nice, harmless little
teacher of ethical platitudes.

The situation is very simple. The claims of Jesus are
either true or false. If they are false, they could be deliberately false (in which case he was a liar, an impostor) or they
could be involuntarily false (in which case he was
deluded). Yet neither possibility appears at all likely. Jesus
hated religious pretence or hypocrisy. He was a person of
such integrity that it is hard to believe he was a charlatan.
As for having a fixed delusion about himself, there

certainly are psychotic people who imagine they are the Queen of Sheba, Julius Caesar, the Emperor of Japan or some other VIP. But one thing is fatal to this theory in regard to Jesus. It is that deluded people delude nobody but themselves. You have only to be in their presence for two or three minutes before you know that they are withdrawn from reality and living in a world of fantasy. But not Jesus. He has succeeded in persuading (or deluding) millions of people, for the very good reason that he seems to be what he claimed to be. There is no dichotomy between his character and his claims.

This dilemma has been forcefully expressed by C. S. Lewis:

> A man who was merely a man and said the sort of things Jesus said would not be a great moral teacher. He would either be a lunatic – on a level with the man who says he is a poached egg – or else he would be the devil of hell. You must make your choice. Either this man was, and is, the Son of God: or else a madman or something worse. You can shut him up for a fool, you can spit at him and kill him as a demon; or you can fall at his feet and call him Lord and God. But let us not come with any patronizing nonsense about his being a great human teacher. He has not left that open to us. He did not intend to.[3]

This is the paradox of Jesus. His claims sound like the ravings of a lunatic, but he shows no sign of being a fanatic, a neurotic or, still less, a psychotic. On the contrary, he comes before us in the pages of the Gospels as the most balanced and integrated of human beings.

Consider in particular his humility. His claims for himself are very disturbing, because they are so self-centred; yet in his behaviour he was clothed with humility. His claims sound proud, but he was humble. I see this paradox at its sharpest when he was with his disciples in the upper room before he died. He said he was their lord, their teacher and their judge, but he took a towel, got on his hands and knees, and washed their feet like a common slave. Is this not unique in the history of the world? There have been lots of arrogant people, but they have all behaved like it. There have also been humble people, but they have not made great claims for themselves. It is the combination of egocentricity and humility that is so startling – the egocentricity of his teaching and the humility of his behaviour.

He said he was their lord, their teacher and their judge, but he took a towel, got on his hands and knees, and washed their feet like a common slave.

Why am I a Christian? Intellectually speaking, it is because of the paradox of Jesus Christ. It is because he who claimed to be his disciples' Lord humbled himself to be their servant.

But God demonstrates his own love for us in this:

While we were still sinners, Christ died for us.

Romans 5:8

Chapter 3

THE CROSS OF CHRIST

From the beginning his followers laid their emphasis on his death.

The claims of Jesus relate not only to who he was but also to what he came into the world to do; not only to his person but to his mission; not only to his life but to his death.

Anybody who investigates Christianity for the first time will be struck by the extraordinary stress his followers put on his death. In the case of all other great spiritual leaders their death is lamented as terminating their career. It is of no importance in itself; what matters is their life, their teaching and the inspiration of their example.

With Jesus, however, it is the other way round. His teaching and example were indeed incomparable, but from

the beginning his followers laid their emphasis on his
death. Take his three greatest apostles, Paul, Peter and John:

> *Paul:* 'I resolved to know nothing while I was with you except
> Jesus Christ and him crucified' (1 Corinthians 2:2).
> *Peter:* 'For Christ died for sins once for all, the righteous for the
> unrighteous, to bring you to God' (1 Peter 3:18).
> *John:* 'This is love: not that we loved God, but that he loved us
> and sent his Son as an atoning sacrifice for our sins' (1 John
> 4:10).

Moreover, when the Gospels came to be written, the four
Gospel-writers devoted a disproportionate amount of
space to the last week of his life on earth – in the case of
Luke a quarter, of Matthew and Mark about a third, and
of John as much as a half.

And the reason for this emphasis by the apostles is that
they had seen it in the mind of Jesus himself. It set him
apart from the other religious leaders in history. They died
of natural causes in a good old age, having successfully
completed their mission. Muhammad was sixty-two,
Confucius seventy-two, the Buddha eighty, and Moses
120. But Jesus died the horrible death of crucifixion in his
early thirties, repudiated by his own people, apparently a
complete failure, yet claiming to fulfil his mission by his
death. Indeed, during his last few days on earth, he was
still looking forward to the accomplishment of his work.

It is clear, then, that Jesus' death was central to his own
self-understanding. On three separate and solemn occasions he predicted his death, saying that 'the Son of Man

must suffer many things ... and ... be killed' (Mark 8:31; cf. 9:31; 10:32–34). He saw his mission as being completed by his death, and therefore his death as inevitable. It *must* take place, he said. He also referred to his death as the 'hour' for which he had come into the world. At first this 'hour' kept being delayed, but at last he could say, 'The hour has come' (John 12:23–24). And finally, during the Thursday evening, while he was taking supper with the Twelve, he deliberately made provision for his own memorial service. They were to take, break and eat bread in memory of his body given for them, and to drink wine in memory of his blood poured out for them. Death speaks to us from both the elements – the broken bread and the poured-out wine. No symbolism could be more dramatic. Thus Jesus gave clear instructions as to how he wished to be remembered: it was for his death.

The broken bread and the poured-out wine. No symbolism could be more dramatic.

So the church has been right to choose the cross as its symbol for Christianity. It could have chosen the crib in which the baby Jesus was laid (as an emblem of the incarnation), or the carpenter's bench (affirming the dignity of manual labour), or the boat from which he taught the people, or the towel with which he washed and wiped the disciples' feet (as symbols of humble service), or the tomb from which he rose again, or the throne he occupies today (representing his sovereignty), or the dove or the fire (emblems of the Holy Spirit). Any one of these could have been an appropriate symbol of the Christian faith. But the church passed them all by in favour of the cross, which stands for the necessity and centrality of his death.

So we see it everywhere. In many churches candidates for baptism are signed with the sign of the cross. And if after our death we are buried, our family and friends will probably erect a tombstone over our grave, on which they will have had a cross inscribed. In the Middle Ages the great cathedrals of Europe were deliberately built on a cruciform ground-plan, the nave and transepts forming a massive cross. And many church members like to declare their Christian identity by wearing a cross on a necklace or pendant. Indeed, to do so is a challenge to one's own Christian commitment. One such was Malcolm Muggeridge:

> I would catch a glimpse of a cross [he wrote in later life], not necessarily a crucifix; maybe two pieces of wood accidentally nailed together, on a telegraph pole, for instance – and suddenly my heart would stand still. In an instinctive, intuitive way I understood that something more important, more tumultuous, more passionate, was at issue than our good causes, however admirable they might be ... It was, I know, an obsessive interest ... I might fasten bits of wood together myself, or doodle it. This symbol, which was considered to be derisory in my home, was yet also the focus of inconceivable hopes and desires ... As I remember this, a sense of my own

failure lies leadenly upon me. I should have worn it over my heart; carried it, a precious standard never to be wrested out of my hands; even though I fell, still borne aloft. It should have been my cult, my uniform, my language, my life. I shall have no excuse; I can't say I didn't know. I knew from the beginning and turned away.[1]

The choice of the cross as the supreme Christian symbol was all the more remarkable because in Greco-Roman culture the cross was an emblem of shame. The Romans reserved the painful and humiliating death by crucifixion for their worst criminals and most dangerous traitors. No Roman citizen was ever crucified. Cicero condemned it as 'a most cruel and disgusting punishment'.[2] And in his famous defence of an elderly senator he insisted that 'the very word "cross" should be far removed not only from the person of a Roman citizen, but from his thoughts, his eyes and his ears'.[3]

Why then this relentless emphasis on the cross? Why did Christ die? Many have no difficulty in giving their answer to these questions. He died, they say, because he was a preacher of subversive doctrines. He was a revolutionary thinker who so disturbed the prejudices of his contemporaries that they had to get rid of him. He died as the victim of small minds, as a martyr to his own greatness.

This martyr-theory is true as far as it goes, but it does not go far enough. It ignores the fact (which the narratives make plain) that he went to the cross of his own free will.

'I am the good shepherd,' he said. 'The good shepherd lays down his life for the sheep ... No-one takes it from me, but I lay it down of my own accord. I have authority to lay it down and authority to take it up again' (John 10:11, 18).

But why did he go voluntarily and deliberately to the cross? Why did he lay down his life for us? Several reasons could be given, for the cross is too rich an event to be given a single explanation. I will select the three major ones the Bible gives:

First, Christ died to atone for our sins.
Second, Christ died to reveal the character of God.
Third, Christ died to conquer the powers of evil.

Or, to use a single word for each explanation, the death of Christ was an atonement, a revelation and a conquest – an atonement for sin, a revelation of God and a conquest of evil.

CHRIST DIED TO ATONE FOR OUR SINS
The cross of Christ is the only basis on which God can forgive sins.

But why, an impatient critic will immediately object, should our forgiveness depend on Christ's death? Why does God not simply forgive us, without the necessity of the cross? 'God will pardon me', Heinrich Heine protested. 'That's his *métier* [his job, his speciality].'[4] After all, the objector might continue, if we sin against each other, we are required to forgive each other. So why should God not practise what he preaches? Why should he not be as generous as he expects us to be?

Two answers need to be given to these questions. The first was given at the end of the eleventh century by Anselm, Archbishop of Canterbury. He wrote in his magnificent book *Why God Became Man*: 'You have not yet considered the seriousness of sin.'[5] The second answer might be: 'You have not yet considered the majesty of God.' To draw an analogy between our forgiveness of each other and God's forgiveness of us is very superficial. We are not God but private individuals, while he is the maker of heaven and earth, Creator of the very laws we break. Our sins are not purely personal injuries but a wilful rebellion against him. It is when we begin to see the gravity of sin and the majesty of God that our questions change. No longer do we ask *why* God finds it difficult to forgive sins, but *how* he finds it possible. As one writer has put it, 'forgiveness is to man the plainest of duties; to God it is the profoundest of problems'.[6]

Why may forgiveness be described as a 'problem' to God? Because of who he is in his innermost being. Of course he is love (1 John 4:8, 16), but his love is not sentimental love; it is holy love. How then could God punish sin (as in justice he must) without contradicting his love? Or how could God pardon sin (as in love he yearned to do) without compromising his justice? How, confronted by human evil, could God be true to himself as holy love? How could he act simultaneously to express his holiness and his love?

This is the divine dilemma that God resolved on the

cross. For on the cross, when Jesus died, God himself in Christ bore the judgment we deserved, in order to bring us the forgiveness we do not deserve. The full penalty of sin was borne – not, however, by us, but by God in Christ. On the cross divine love and justice were reconciled.

All this wonderful truth is encapsulated in the Bible's simple, often repeated statement, 'Christ died for our sins.' Sin and death are constantly bracketed, even riveted, through the pages of the Bible. From Genesis 2 (verse 17) to Revelation 21 (verse 8) the same truth is hammered home that 'the wages of sin is death' (Romans 6:23), that is, that they separate us from God. Normally, the sin and the death are ours. We sin, and we die. But when the apostles are writing about the cross, they make the amazing statement that *Christ* died for *our* sins. That is, the sin was ours, but now the death (or alienation from God), which is the penalty for sin, was his. This is what is meant by a 'substitutionary' atonement. He took our place, bore our sin, paid our debt and died our death. And if we ask how Christ died our death, we can only point to those three hours of God-forsaken darkness in which Christ tasted the desolation of hell in our place, that we might be spared it.

Christ tasted the desolation of hell in our place, that we might be spared it.

CHRIST DIED TO REVEAL THE CHARACTER OF GOD

If Christ died to atone for our sins, he also died to reveal the character of God. For just as we human beings disclose our character by our actions, so does God. He has shown himself to us supremely by giving his Son to die for us.

Twice in his great letter to the Romans, Paul wrote of the demonstration, even the vindication, of God's character of justice and love in the cross. It may be helpful, before we study these two key texts separately, to set them side by side:

> God ... did this [i.e. presented Christ as a sacrifice of atonement] to demonstrate his justice, because in his forbearance he had left the sins committed beforehand unpunished – he did it to demonstrate his justice at the present time, so as to be just and the one who justifies those who have faith in Jesus (Romans 3:25–26).

> But God demonstrates his own love for us in this: While we were still sinners, Christ died for us (Romans 5:8).

In these two texts Paul declares that in and through the death of Jesus Christ God has given a clear, public demonstration of both his justice and his love.

I take *God's justice* first. Men and women of moral sensitivity have always been perplexed by the seeming injustices of God's providence. It is one of the recurring themes of the biblical wisdom literature, and it dominates the book of Job. Why do the wicked flourish, and why do the innocent suffer? There is evidently need for a 'theodicy', that is, a vindication of the justice of God, a justification to humankind of the apparently unjust ways of God.

The Bible responds to this need in two ways. First, it points us to the future final judgment, when all wrongs will be righted, and meanwhile it points us back to the decisive judgment that took place on the cross. For there God himself in Christ bore the penalty of our sins. Thus the reason for God's previous inaction in the face of evil was not his moral indifference but his patient forbearance until Christ should come and deal with it by his death. No-one can now accuse God of condoning evil and so of injustice.

> *How can the sum total of human misery be reconciled with a God of love?*

But what about *God's love*? How can we believe in the love of God when there seems to be so much evidence against it? I am thinking of personal tragedies and natural disasters, worldwide poverty and hunger, tyranny and torture, disease and death. How can the sum total of human misery be reconciled with a God of love?

Christianity offers no glib answer to these agonized questions. But it does offer evidence of God's love, which is just as historical and objective as the evidence that seems to deny it, namely the cross. The cross does not explain calamity, but it gives us a vantage ground from which to view it and bear it.

In order to understand this, we need to return to Romans 5:8 and the demonstration of God's love: 'But God demonstrates his own love for us in this: While we were still sinners, Christ died for us.' This demonstration is of 'his own love for us'. It is unique, for there is no other love like it. It has three parts, which together build a convincing case.

Firstly, God gave *his Son* for us. True, in Romans 5:8 Paul affirms simply that 'Christ' died for us. But the context tells us who this Christ, the Messiah, was. According to verse 10, Christ's death was 'the death of his [God's] Son'. So in sending Christ God was not sending someone else, a creature, a third party. No, in sending his own Son he was giving himself.

Secondly, God gave his Son *to die* for us. It would still have been wonderful if God had given his Son, and so himself, only to become a human being for us. But he went further, 'even to death on a cross' (Philippians 2:7–8), to the torture of crucifixion and to the horror of sin-bearing and God-forsakenness. We have no means of imagining the appalling pain involved in such experiences.

Thirdly, God gave his Son to die *for us*, that is, for people Paul goes on to describe as 'sinners', 'ungodly', 'enemies' and 'powerless' (Romans 5:6–10). Very rarely, Paul continues, somebody may be willing to die for a 'righteous' man (whose righteousness is cold, austere and forbidding), though for a 'good' man (whose goodness is warm, friendly and attractive) somebody might possibly dare to die. But God demonstrates his own unique love for us in this: that he died for sinful, godless, rebellious and helpless people like us.

The value of a love-gift is assessed both by what it costs the giver and by the degree to which the recipient may be held to deserve it. A young man in love will give his beloved expensive presents because he considers that she deserves them. But God, in giving his Son, gave himself to die for his enemies. He gave everything for those who deserved nothing from him. And that is God's own proof of his love for us. So what we have been given in the sin-bearing death of Jesus Christ is not a solution to the problem of pain, but sure and solid evidence of both the justice and the love of God, in the light of which we may learn to live and love, to serve, to suffer and to die.

CHRIST DIED TO CONQUER THE POWERS OF EVIL

If Christ died to atone for our sins and to reveal the character of God, he also died to conquer the powers of evil. Indeed, it is impossible to read the New Testament without being struck by the atmosphere of joyful confidence that pervades it and that stands out in relief against the rather insipid religion that often passes for Christianity today. There was no defeatism about the early Christians; they spoke rather of victory. For example: 'Thanks be to God! He gives us the victory through our

Lord Jesus Christ' (1 Corinthians 15:57); 'In all these things [that is, adversities and dangers] we are more than conquerors' (Romans 8:37).

Victory, conquest, triumph, overcoming – this was the vocabulary of those first followers of Jesus. They attributed this victory to the cross.

Yet any contemporary observer who saw Christ die would have listened with astonished incredulity to the claim that the Crucified was a Conqueror. Had he not been rejected by his own nation, betrayed, denied and deserted by his own disciples, and executed by authority of the Roman procurator? Look at him there, spread-eagled and skewered on his cross, robbed of all freedom of movement, strung up with nails or ropes or both, pinned there and powerless. It appears to be total defeat. If there is victory, it is the victory of pride, prejudice, jealousy, hatred, cowardice and brutality.

Yet the Christian claim is that the reality is the opposite of the appearance. What looked like (and in one sense was) the defeat of goodness by evil, is also, and more certainly, the defeat of evil by goodness. Overcome there, he was himself overcoming. Crushed by the ruthless power of Rome, he was himself crushing the serpent's head (as was predicted in Genesis 3:15). The victim was the victor, and the cross is still the throne from which he rules the world.

In vivid imagery the apostle Paul describes how the powers of evil surrounded Jesus and closed in round him on the cross, how he stripped them from himself, disarmed them and made a public spectacle of them, triumphing over them by the cross (Colossians 2:15). What precise form this cosmic battle took is not explained. But we do know that Jesus resisted the temptation to avoid the cross, and instead became obedient to it; that, when provoked by insults and tortures, he absolutely refused to retaliate, thus overcoming evil with good (Romans 12:21); and that, when the combined forces of Jerusalem and Rome were arrayed against him, he declined any resort to worldly power. Thus he refused to disobey God, to hate his enemies or to imitate the world's use of power. By his obedience, love and meekness he won a decisive moral victory over the powers of darkness. He remained free, uncontaminated and uncompromised. This was his victory. The devil could gain no hold on him, and was obliged to concede defeat.

We are not, therefore, to regard the cross as defeat and the resurrection as victory. Rather, the cross was the victory won, and the resurrection the victory endorsed, proclaimed and demonstrated.

This theme of victory through the cross, which the ancient Greek fathers and later Latin fathers celebrated, was lost by some medieval theologians but recovered by Martin Luther at the Reformation. This was the thesis of Gustav Aulén, a Swedish theologian, in his influential book *Christus Victor* (1930). He was right to remind the church of this somewhat neglected motif. Yet we must not make the opposite mistake, so emphasizing the theme of triumph that we forget the themes of atonement and revelation. In any balanced understanding of the cross, we shall confess Christ as saviour (atoning for our sins), as teacher (disclosing the character of God) and as victor (overcoming the powers of evil).

Why am I a Christian? One reason is the cross of Christ. Indeed, I could never myself believe in God if it were not for the cross. It is the cross that gives God his credibility. The only God I believe in is the one Nietzsche (the nineteenth-century German philosopher) ridiculed as 'God on the cross'. In the real world of pain, how could one worship a God who was immune to it?

I could never myself believe in God if it were not for the cross.

In the course of my travels I have entered a number of Buddhist temples in different Asian countries. I have stood respectfully before a statue of the Buddha, his legs crossed, arms folded, eyes closed, the ghost of a smile playing round his mouth, serene and silent, a remote look on his face, detached from the agonies of the world. But each time after a while I have had to turn away. And in my imagination I have turned instead to that lonely, twisted, tortured figure on the cross, nails through hands and feet, back lacerated, limbs wrenched, brow bleeding from thorn-pricks, mouth dry and intolerably thirsty, plunged in God-forsaken darkness.

The crucified one is the God for me! He laid aside his immunity to pain. He entered our world of flesh and blood, tears and death. He suffered for us, dying in our place in order that we might be forgiven. Our sufferings become more manageable in the light of his. There is still a question-mark against human suffering, but over it we boldly stamp another mark, the cross, which symbolizes divine suffering.

'The cross of Christ ... is God's only self-justification in such a world' as ours.[7]

So God created man

in his own image,

in the image of God

he created him;

male and female

he created them.

GENESIS 1:27

Chapter 4

THE PARADOX OF
OUR HUMANNESS

Why am I a Christian? Not only because Christianity explains who Jesus was, and what he achieved on the cross, but because it also explains who I am. Twice in the Bible the question is asked, and to some degree answered: 'What is man?' (Psalm 8:4; Job 7:17). That is, what does it mean to be a human being? What is the essence of our humanness?

There are three reasons why this question is of great importance – personal, political and professional.

First, *personal.* To ask, 'What is man?' is another way of asking, 'Who am I?' It enables us to respond both to the ancient Greek formula *gnōthi seauton* ('know yourself') and to the modern quest for our own identity. There is no more important field for search and research than this.

Until we have discovered ourselves we cannot easily discover anything else.

A story is told of Artur Schopenhauer, the nineteenth-century German philosopher of pessimism. One day he was sitting on a bench in a Frankfurt park. He looked shabby and dishevelled (as western philosophers sometimes do!), so that the park-keeper mistook him for a tramp. He asked him gruffly, 'Who are you?', to which the philosopher replied bitterly, 'I would to God I knew.'

Douglas Coupland asked the same question. He was the inventor of the popular expression 'Generation X' – 'X' standing for the unknown identity of his generation. 'They don't have a name,' he wrote, 'they're an "X" generation.' So 'What makes humans ... human?', he asked. 'We know what dog behaviour is: dogs do doggy things – they chase sticks ... they stick their heads out of moving car windows.' So we know the dogginess of dogs; but 'what exactly is it that *humans* do that is specifically human?'[1] Again, 'What is the *you* of *you*?', that is, the real you?[2]

> *Until we have discovered ourselves we cannot easily discover anything else.*

Many answers have been given to this question, especially to the question wherein the *superiority* of human beings is to be found. It is amusing to review some of the answers given. A human being was described by Aristotle as a political animal, by Thomas Willis as a laughing animal, by Benjamin Franklin as a tool-making animal, by Edmund Burke as a religious animal, and by James Boswell (the gourmet) as a cooking animal.

Other writers have focused on some physical feature as our distinguishing characteristic. Plato made much of our erect posture, so that animals look down, while only human beings look up to heaven. Aristotle added the peculiarity that only human beings are unable to wiggle their ears. A Stuart doctor, however, was greatly impressed by our intestines, by their 'anfractuous circumlocutions, windings and turnings'. Then in the late eighteenth century Uvedale Price drew special attention to our nose. 'Man is, I believe', he wrote, 'the only animal that has a marked projection in the middle of the face.'[3]

None of these descriptions of our distinctiveness gives a complete picture, however, nor do they get to the heart of the matter.

We turn now from the personal to the *political* importance of the question about our humanness. The chief point of conflict between the rival ideologies of Marx and Jesus remains the nature of human beings. 'Ideologies ... are really anthropologies', wrote J. S. Whale; they are different doctrines of man.[4] That is, do human beings have an absolute value, because of which they must be respected? Or is their value only relative to the State, because of which they may be exploited? More simply, are people the servants of the institution, or is the institution the servant of the people?

Thirdly, our question has a *professional* importance. The great professions (e.g. in education and the law) and the so-called 'caring' professions (in medical, paramedical and social work) are all concerned with the welfare of human beings, whether they call them patients, pupils or clients. And how they treat those they serve depends almost entirely on how they evaluate them.

Having considered the importance of our question (personal, political and professional), we return to the question itself. The Christian critique of much modern philosophy and ideology is that it is either too naïve in its optimism about the human condition or too negative in its pessimism, whereas we dare to add that only the Bible keeps the balance.

Secular humanists tend to be very optimistic. True, they declare that human beings are nothing but the product of blind evolutionary forces. But they have boundless confidence in what they regard as our future evolutionary potential, especially that one day human beings will be able to take hold of their own history and control their own destiny. But that is too optimistic. It does not take into account what Christians call 'original sin', which is a twist of self-centredness in our nature and which has repeatedly thwarted the dreams of social reformers.

Atheistic existentialists, on the other hand, go to the opposite extreme of pessimism, even of despair. Because there is no God, they say, there are no longer any values. Although we must somehow find the courage to be, nothing has meaning and everything is ultimately absurd – which is at least logical if God is dead. Mark Twain, the famous American wit, although he lived long before the development of existentialism, nevertheless expressed a kind of existential cynicism when he said, 'If man could be crossed with the cat, it would improve man, but it would deteriorate the cat!'[5] But this is too pessimistic. It takes no account of the love, joy, beauty, heroism and self-sacrifice that have adorned the human story.

It is my contention that only authentic Christianity avoids both extremes, for what we need, to quote J. S. Whale again, is 'neither the easy optimism of the humanist, nor the dark pessimism of the cynic, but the radical realism of the Bible'.[6] For the Bible preserves the paradox, namely the glory and the shame of our humanness, our dignity and our depravity.

1. THE GLORY

It is in the very first chapter of the Bible that we hear the majestic words of God:

'Let us make man in our image, in our likeness, and let them rule over the fish of the sea and the birds of the air, over the livestock, over all the earth, and over all the creatures that move along the ground.'

So God created man
    in his own image,
in the image of God
    he created him;

> male and female
>   he created them.
>   (Genesis 1:26–27)

There has been much discussion about the meaning of the divine image in human beings. Some scholars emphasize that in the cultures of Egypt and Assyria the king or emperor was regarded as 'the image of God', representing him on earth, and that they had images of themselves erected in their provinces to symbolize the extent of their jurisdiction. Against this background God has entrusted a royal responsibility to human beings, appointing them to rule over the earth and its creatures.

In the unfolding narrative of the Bible, however, the divine image is clearly what distinguishes humans from animals, namely a cluster of unique human qualities.

First, there is *our capacity for rational thought*. Of course, animals also have brains, some more rudimentary than others. But they lack 'understanding' or intelligence (Psalm 32:9), whereas human beings are able to think, reason, argue and debate. We are also self-conscious. That is, we have the extraordinary ability to do what we are doing at this moment, namely to step outside ourselves, to evaluate ourselves, and to ask ourselves questions about our own identity. It is true that, astronomically speaking, as one scientist said to another, man is extremely insignificant. But then, astronomically speaking, his colleague responded, man is the astronomer! We are restlessly inquisitive about the universe. As Archbishop William

Temple once said, 'I am greater than the stars, for I know that they are up there, but they do not know that I am down here.'

Secondly, there is *our capacity for moral choice.* We have a conscience to discern between good and evil, together with a degree of freedom to choose between them. We are aware of a moral order outside and above us, to which we know we are accountable, so that we have an inner urge to do what we believe to be right, and a profound sense of guilt when we do what we know to be wrong.

But animals have no moral sense. For instance, you can train your dog (by repetitive punishments and rewards) to obey your commands and to learn that it is allowed to sit on only one chair in the lounge. If on entering the room you find it sitting on a forbidden seat, it will instinctively cower away from you, not because it feels guilty (however guilty it may look) but because it knows it's going to be smacked.

Thirdly, there is *our capacity for artistic creativity.* When God created us in his own image, he made us creative like himself. We are 'creative creatures'. So we draw and we paint, we build and we sculpt, we dream and we dance, we write poetry and we make music. Human beings are both imaginative and innovative. We appreciate what is beautiful to the eye, the ear and the touch.

Fourthly, there is *our capacity for social relationships.* Of course, all animals mate and reproduce, and care for their young. While some are gregarious (going about in flocks or herds), others develop highly complex social structures (e.g. bees, wasps and ants). But human beings hunger for the authentic relationships of love. Love is not just a disturbance in the endocrine glands! Everybody knows that love is the greatest thing in the world. Living is loving, and without love the human personality disintegrates and dies. Moreover, Christians know why love is pre-eminent. It is because God is love in his innermost being, so that when he made us in his image he gave us the capacity to love and to be loved.

> *Without love the human personality disintegrates and dies.*

Fifthly, there is *our capacity for humble worship.* There has been much discussion about the collapse of Euro-Marxism and its causes. Many believe it was due to its gross materialism. For materialism cannot satisfy the human spirit either in its communistic or in its capitalistic form. We know instinctively that there is a transcendent reality beyond the material order, and people are seeking it everywhere. The New Age movement is perhaps one evidence of this quest. Human beings do not live – indeed, cannot live – on bread alone, Jesus said, quoting from the Old Testament (Matthew 4:4; Deuteronomy 8:3), or, as Dostoyevski wrote, 'man must bow down before the infinitely great'. We are most truly human when we are worshipping God.

Here then, are five human capacities (to think, choose, create, love and worship) that set us apart from animals and that together constitute the image of God in us. No wonder poets and dramatists have celebrated the unique dignity of human beings. Hamlet was hardly exaggerating when he said to himself, 'What a piece of work is man! How noble in reason! how infinite in faculties! ... in action how like an angel! in apprehension, how like a god! the beauty of the world! the paragon of animals!'[7]

How I wish I could end this chapter here, and we could move on to the next topic, glowing with unadulterated self-esteem! But there is another and darker side to our humanness, which we wish we could forget, but which keeps reasserting itself and of which in our best moments we are thoroughly ashamed. As Mark Twain put it: 'Man is the only animal that blushes. Or needs to.'[8]

2. THE SHAME
Jesus himself spoke of this. Here is perhaps his most outspoken statement:

> 'For from within, out of men's hearts, come evil thoughts, sexual immorality, theft, murder, adultery, greed, malice, deceit, lewdness, envy, slander, arrogance and folly. All these evils come from inside and make a man "unclean"' (Mark 7:21–23).

So Jesus did not teach the fundamental goodness of human nature; on the contrary, he insisted on our innate human capacity for evil. Indeed, in this passage there are four aspects of human evil that should engage our attention.

Firstly, *the extent of evil is universal.* We note that Jesus was not describing the criminal segment of society, or some particularly degraded tribe. No, he was talking with those religious and righteous people called Pharisees. And he made a general statement about the whole human race, namely that out of the heart of man (any and every man, woman and child) evil things come.

Secondly, *the essence of evil is self-centredness.* We have already noted this. Now Jesus gives a list of thirteen 'evils' and, when we study them, they are all manifestations of human self-centredness. They are the thoughts, words and deeds of which we become guilty when we fail to put God first, our neighbour next and ourselves last. I once took down the *Shorter Oxford English Dictionary* and looked up the words compounded with 'self' – words like self-assertion, self-indulgence, self-applause, self-advertisement, self-gratification, self-glorification, self-pity and self-will. There are more than fifty self-words that have a pejorative meaning. We evidently need this rich vocabulary to express our multifaceted self-centredness.

> *The heart of the human problem is the problem of the human heart.*

Thirdly, *the origin of evil is the human heart.* As has often been said, 'the heart of the human problem is the problem of the human heart'. The Pharisees, with whom Jesus was in debate, had an external and ceremonial view of defilement and purity. They were concerned for the washing of hands and vessels, and the avoidance of certain foods. But Jesus emphasized not the external but the internal. What defiles us is not what goes into us (into our stomach) but what comes out of us (out of our heart).

One might almost say that Jesus was introducing us to Freudianism centuries before Freud. For what Jesus called the heart is roughly equivalent to what Freud called the subconscious. It is like a very deep well. Normally the thick deposit of mud at the bottom is unseen and unsuspected. But when the waters of the well are stirred by the winds of violent emotion, the most evil-looking, evil-smelling filth bubbles up from the depths and breaks the surface – anger, malice, lust, hatred, cruelty and revenge – and we are horrified to glimpse the evils of which our heart is capable.

Fourthly, *the result of evil is that it defiles us.* That is, it makes us unclean in the sight of God and unfit for his presence. All those who have caught even a momentary glimpse of God's holiness have not been able to bear the sight – like Moses at the burning bush, who 'hid his face, because he was afraid to look at God' (Exodus 3:6).

This, then, is the shame of our humanness. Human evil is universal in its extent, self-centred in its nature, inward in its origin and defiling in its effect. This is not only the diagnosis of (arguably) the greatest ethical teacher in history, but it is also true to our own experience. It is certainly true of mine.

3. THE PARADOX

Now we are ready to bring together the glory and the shame, the dignity and the depravity, of our humanness. For human beings are a strange and tragic paradox. We are capable of both the loftiest nobility and the basest cruelty. We are able to behave at one moment like God, in whose image we were made, and in the next moment like the beasts, from whom we were meant to be for ever distinct. We are able to think, choose, create, love and worship; but we are also able to hate, covet, fight and kill. Human beings are the inventors of hospitals for the care of the sick, of universities for the acquisition of wisdom, and of churches for the worship of God. But they have also invented torture chambers, concentration camps and nuclear arsenals.

This is the paradox of our humanness. We are both noble and ignoble, both rational and irrational, both moral and immoral, both creative and destructive, both loving and selfish, both God-like and bestial.

I know no more eloquent statement of the human paradox than one given a good many years ago by Bishop Richard Holloway:

> This is my dilemma ... I am dust and ashes, frail and wayward, a set of predetermined behavioural responses ... riddled with fears, beset with needs ... the quintessence of dust and unto dust I shall return ... *But* there is something else in me ... Dust I may be, but troubled dust, dust that dreams, dust that has strange premonitions of transfiguration, of a glory in store, a destiny prepared, an inheritance that will one day be my own

... So my life is stretched out in a painful dialectic between ashes and glory, between weakness and transfiguration. I am a riddle to myself, an exasperating enigma ... this strange duality of dust and glory.[9]

The paradox of our humanness has a number of practical consequences – especially political, psychological and personal.

Politically, the human paradox or ambiguity makes democracy the best form of government yet developed. For ideally democracy recognizes both the dignity and the depravity of our human being. On the one hand, it recognizes our human dignity, because it refuses to push people around or to govern us without our consent. Instead, it gives us a share in the decision-making process. It treats us with respect as responsible adults.

> *Democracy recognizes both the dignity and the depravity of our human being.*

On the other hand, democracy also recognizes our human depravity. For it refuses to concentrate power in the hands of a few, knowing that it is not safe to do so. So it is of the essence of democracy to disperse power and so protect rulers from themselves. As Reinhold Niebuhr put it, 'man's capacity for justice makes democracy possible;

but man's inclination to injustice makes democracy necessary'.[10]

I come secondly to the *psychological* consequences of the human paradox. We all know the importance for our mental health of having a balanced self-image. Some people have crippling inferiority feelings and a very poor self-image. Others go to the opposite extreme. Carl Rogers, for example, the American founder of 'client-centred psychotherapy', came to believe that the core of our human personality is positive, and that we need therefore to develop an 'unconditional positive self-regard'.[11] This kind of thinking flourishes in the self-actualization movement and has overtaken many Christians, who argue that we are to love God, our neighbour and ourselves. But this means we are to love our neighbour as in fact, being fallen, we do love ourselves. It is not an exhortation to love ourselves, as is clear from three arguments. First, Jesus spoke of the first and second commandments, but did not mention a third. Secondly, self-love is the very essence of sin (2 Timothy 3:2). Thirdly, the love that is to characterize our lives is *agapē* love, which includes both sacrifice and service, and therefore cannot be turned in on ourselves. How can we sacrifice ourselves to serve ourselves?

What, then, is a balanced self-image? If we are neither to hate ourselves nor to love ourselves, how are we to regard ourselves? It is here that the human paradox comes in. We are to remember that human beings are the product of both the creation and the fall. So, then, everything in us that is attributable to our creation in the image of God we gratefully affirm, while everything in us that is attributable to the fall we must resolutely repudiate or deny. Thus we are called both to self-affirmation and to self-denial, and we need discernment to distinguish which is appropriate and when.

The third consequence of the human paradox is *personal.* We have seen that Jesus describes evil as both issuing from our heart and causing our defilement. It is clear therefore from this that we have a double need: on the one hand cleansing from defilement, and on the other a new heart with new desires and aspirations. And to me it is truly wonderful that both these are offered to us in the gospel. For Christ died to make us clean, and by the inward working of his Holy Spirit he can make us new. This is the logical application of the gospel in response to the paradox of our humanness; it is the fourth reason why I am a Christian.

Human beings are the product of both the creation and the fall.

———————————————

So if the Son sets you free, you will be free indeed.

———————————————

JOHN 8:36

Chapter 5

THE KEY TO FREEDOM

The fifth reason why I am a Christian is that I have found Jesus Christ to be the key to freedom.

Many people are preoccupied with a quest for freedom. For some it is national freedom, emancipation from a colonial or neo-colonial yoke. For others it is civil freedom, civil rights and civil liberties. For others it is economic freedom, freedom from poverty, hunger and unemployment. But for all of us it is personal freedom. Even those who campaign most vigorously for those other freedoms often know that they are not free themselves. They feel frustrated, unfulfilled and unfree. John Fowles, the celebrated British novelist, was once asked if there was any special theme in his books. 'Yes,' he replied. 'Freedom. How you achieve freedom. That obsesses me. All my books are about that.'[1]

And freedom is a great Christian word. Jesus Christ is portrayed in the New Testament as the world's supreme liberator. He had come, he said, 'to proclaim freedom for the prisoners' (Luke 4:18), and added later that 'if the Son sets you free, you will be free indeed' (John 8:36). Similarly, the apostle Paul wrote, 'It is for freedom that Christ has set us free' (Galatians 5:1).

Now freedom is a good modern word for 'salvation'. To be saved by Jesus Christ is to be set free. Drop the word 'salvation' into a conversation, however, and it gives off very different vibrations. Some react with embarrassment and change the subject as quickly as possible. Others react with boredom. They yawn rather than blush, for to them the terms 'sin' and 'salvation' belong to a traditional religious vocabulary that is now obsolete and meaningless. A third group are covered with confusion, because they have no idea how 'salvation' should be defined. Talk about 'freedom', however, and people's interest is immediately aroused.

A delightful story, which illustrates this confusion, has long been told of B. F. Westcott, a New Testament scholar of great distinction, who was for some years Regius Professor of Divinity at Cambridge University, and became in 1890 Bishop of Durham. It is said that, while travelling somewhere by bus, he was accosted by a Salvation Army lassie. Undeterred by his lordship's gaiters (bishops wore them in those days!), she asked him if he was saved. With a twinkle in his eye the bishop replied: 'Well, my dear, it depends what you mean. Do you mean *sōzomenos* or *sesōsmenos* or *sōthēsomenos?*' – using the present, past and future tenses of the Greek verb *sōzō*, 'to save'.

My hope in this chapter is that I will not embarrass, bore or confuse you, but rather that we may reclaim and reinstate this great and glorious word 'salvation'; for it is a biblical word (it cannot simply be jettisoned) and a big word (it includes the whole purpose of God). Then we should be able to echo what Paul wrote: 'I am not ashamed of the gospel, because it is the power of God for the salvation of everyone who believes' (Romans 1:16).

I well remember, as a very new Christian, being shown this verse and being introduced to what are called 'the three tenses of salvation'. They go like this:

Firstly, I have been saved (or freed) in the past from the penalty of sin by a crucified Saviour.
Secondly, I am being saved (or freed) in the present from the power of sin by a living Saviour.
Thirdly, I shall be saved (or freed) in the future from the presence of sin by a coming Saviour.

It is a simple structure, which encapsulates what the Bible means by 'salvation'; and it enables us, whenever the word occurs, to ask ourselves which tense of salvation is in mind: past, present or future. The fact that we have been saved frees us from guilt and from God's judgment. The fact that we are being saved frees us from bondage to our own self-centredness. And the fact that we shall be saved frees us from all fear about the future.

1. FREEDOM FROM

First, then, salvation means *freedom from guilt and from the judgment of God.* For we are not only sinners, but guilty sinners, and our conscience tells us so. Moreover, our sin provokes God's wrath and brings us under his just judgment. This is unfashionable language today, but mainly because it is misunderstood. The wrath of God has never meant that he is malicious, bad-tempered or vindictive, but rather that he hates evil and refuses to compromise with it.

We should be thankful that there is a considerable reaction nowadays against Freud's teaching that guilt feelings are pathological, symptoms of mental sickness. Indeed, some *are* pathological, especially in some forms of depressive illness. But many – perhaps most – are not. Not all guilt is false guilt. A number of psychologists and psychotherapists are now telling us, even if they make no Christian profession themselves, that we must take our responsibilities seriously. Then (if we fail to do so) our guilt and our need of forgiveness remain.

Nobody is free who is unforgiven.

Nobody is free who is unforgiven. If I were not sure of God's forgiveness, I could not look you in the face, and I certainly could not look God in the face. I would want to run away and hide, as Adam and Eve did in the Garden of Eden. For it was in Eden, not at Watergate, that the device called 'cover-up' was first invented. I would not be free. Yet we long for the freedom that forgiveness brings. Not long before she died in 1988, in a moment of surprising candour on television, Marghanita Laski, one of Britain's leading novelists and atheists, blurted out: 'What I envy most about you Christians is your forgiveness; I have nobody to forgive me.'

'But', as David cried out in Psalm 130:4, 'with you there is forgiveness.' The only way by which we can be set free from guilt and judgment is through Jesus Christ. For when he entered our world, he became one of us, assuming our nature, and on the cross he identified himself with our sin and guilt. In total self-sacrificial love he paid the penalty of our sins. We deserve to die – he died our death in our place. In the awful darkness of the cross he even tasted the horrors of hell, in order that we might go to heaven. It takes a hard and stony heart not to be moved by such amazing love.

Secondly, salvation means *freedom from the cramping bondage of our own self-centredness.* I still remember what a revelation it was to me, as a young man, to learn (mainly through the teaching of Archbishop William Temple) that sin is self, and salvation is freedom from self. Sin is the rebellious assertion of myself against the love and authority of God, and against the welfare of my neighbour. God's order is that we put him first, our neighbour next and self last. Sin is precisely the reversal of the order – me first, neighbour next (when it suits my convenience), and God somewhere (if anywhere) in the distant background.

Luther's favourite definition of a sinner was *homo in se incurvatus*, 'man curved in on himself', and in our day

Malcolm Muggeridge frequently spoke of the 'dark little dungeon of my own ego'. For Jesus once said to some Jewish believers, 'I tell you the truth, everyone who sins is a slave to sin' (John 8:34).

Christians believe there is only one way to be rid of this imprisonment or slavery, and that is through Jesus Christ. He not only died but was raised from death and now lives 'in the power of his resurrection' (see Ephesians 1:19–20; Romans 8:11). For the living Jesus by his Spirit can enter our personality, establish himself there as our permanent guest, subdue our sinful desires and transform us into his own likeness from one degree of glory to another (2 Corinthians 3:18). I am not of course claiming a complete deliverance from all self-centredness. But I am claiming a substantial change from self to unself.

And we have to be willing for it. During a mission in a Canadian university some years ago I found myself talking to a young lecturer. I was trying to explain to him that, if he were to accept Jesus Christ, he would have to put him at the centre of his life and himself move out to the circumference. 'Gee!' he blurted out, 'I guess I'm very reluctant for this de-centralization!'

Thirdly, salvation is *freedom from our crippling fears*. Those who lived in the ancient world were paralysed by fear. They believed that certain 'powers' dominated their lives and their destiny. Many people are similarly haunted by fear today. There are the common fears that have always plagued humankind: fears of sickness, pain, disability and incapacity, the fears of unemployment, financial misfortune and bereavement. Then there are occult powers, the principalities and powers of darkness, for which it is right to have a healthy fear. There are also irrational and superstitious fears. Educated people in Europe still cross their fingers and touch wood. In West Africa they carry jujus (charms). And in North America they refuse to sleep on the thirteenth floor of a high-rise hotel, apparently oblivious of the fact that it is still the thirteenth even if you call it the fourteenth! Education and superstition do not seem to exclude each other. As for the British, one National Opinion Poll revealed that twice as many of us read our horoscope each week as our Bible.

I single out for special mention the fear of death. One New Testament author refers to 'those who all their lives were held in slavery by their fear of death', but now have been set free (Hebrews 2:15). If this writer were addressing our contemporary society, he would not need to change a single word. Apart from Jesus Christ, the fear of death and dissolution is extremely widespread. For us in the West, Woody Allen typifies this terror. It has become an obsession with him. True, he can still joke about it. 'It's not that I'm afraid to die,' he famously quips. 'I just don't want to be there when it happens.'[2] But mostly he is filled with dread. In a 1977 article in *Esquire* he wrote: 'The fundamental thing behind *all* motivation and *all* activity is the constant struggle against annihilation and against death. It's absolutely stupefying in its terror, and it renders anyone's accomplishments meaningless.'[3]

Bertrand Russell tried to put a brave face on his

stoicism, but seems to have had no basis for it: 'I believe that when I die I shall rot, and nothing of my ego will survive.'[4] Again, he affirmed his conviction that

> no fire, no heroism, no intensity of thought and feeling, can preserve an individual life beyond the grave; that all the labours of the ages, all the devotion, all the inspiration, all the noonday brightness of human genius are destined for extinction in the vast death of the solar system, and that the whole temple of man's achievement must inevitably be buried beneath the debris of a universe in ruins.[5]

Reviewing these many human fears, none seems greater than this ultimate threat of personal and cosmic extinction, whether its form will be nuclear, ecological or unknown. One thing is sure: no-one who is afraid is free. And Jesus Christ holds the key to freedom, because he died to free us from guilt, rose to free us from self and was exalted to free us from fear. Where then are the things we fear? God has put them under the feet of Jesus Christ (see Ephesians 1:20–22). Once we have seen them there, they lose their power to terrify. Their spell has been broken. I have been learning that fears are like fungus; they grow most rapidly in the dark. We need, therefore, to bring them out into the light, especially into the light of the supreme victory of Jesus Christ – his death, resurrection and exaltation.

Christians have been given a beautiful confidence about the future, for our Christian 'hope' (which is a sure expectation) is both individual and cosmic. Individually, we are promised resurrection bodies like Jesus' body after his resurrection, and they will have new, undreamed-of powers. Our hope for the future, however, will be cosmic too. We believe that Jesus Christ is going to return in a cosmic event of spectacular magnificence. He will not only raise the dead but regenerate the universe; he will make all things new. The whole creation is going to be set free from its present bondage to decay and death. The groans of nature are the labour pains which promise the birth of a new earth. There is going to be a new heaven and a new earth, which will be the home of righteousness, joy, peace and love (see Romans 8:18–25; 2 Peter 3:13).

So then, the living hope of the New Testament is a 'material' expectation for both the individual and the cosmos. The individual believer is promised neither just survival nor even immortality, but a resurrected, transformed body. And the destiny of the cosmos is not an ethereal 'heaven' but a re-created universe. And the resurrection of Jesus is the ground of both expectations.

He will make all things new.

2. FREEDOM FOR

We have seen what Christ sets us free *from* (the negative aspect of freedom). But whenever we are thinking about freedom, it is important to think of what we are set free *for* as well (the positive aspect).

Let me now develop this thesis, that true freedom is freedom to be one's true self, as God made us and meant us to be. We begin with God himself. God is the only being who enjoys perfect freedom. You could argue that his freedom is not perfect. It is certainly not absolute in the sense that he is free to do absolutely anything whatsoever. There are several things that Scripture itself says God 'cannot' do. He cannot lie. He cannot sin. He cannot tempt and he cannot be tempted. So his freedom is not absolute. But it is perfect, because he is free to do anything that he wills to do. The things God cannot do all come under the general ruling that he cannot deny or contradict himself (2 Timothy 2:13). He is always entirely himself. There is nothing arbitrary, nothing capricious, nothing impulsive in God. He is always the same.

Absolute freedom, freedom unlimited, is an illusion.

He never changes. He is steadfast and immovable. And he finds his freedom in being his true self as God. If he were to contradict himself, he would destroy himself and so cease to be God. But instead he remains himself and never deviates from being himself. What would the universe be like if God were to deviate for a moment from being entirely himself?

Now let us move on from God the Creator to all his creatures, and we will find the same principle operating. Absolute freedom, freedom unlimited, is an illusion, an impossibility. The freedom of every creature is limited by its own created nature. Take as an obvious example a fish. God created fish to live and thrive in water. Their gills are adapted to absorb oxygen from water. They find their freedom to be themselves within the element in which a fish finds its fishiness, its identity, its freedom. Mind you, water imposes a limitation upon fish, but in that limitation is liberty. Its freedom is to be itself within the limits which the Creator has imposed upon it. Supposing you have at home one of those old-fashioned, probably Victorian, spherical goldfish bowls. And supposing your little goldfish swims round and round its blessed bowl until it finds its frustration unbearable, and it determines to make a bid for freedom by leaping out of its bowl. If it should somehow manage to land in a pond in your garden, it would increase its freedom. It is still in water, but there is more water to swim in. But if instead it were to land on concrete or a carpet, its bid for freedom would spell death. Fish can find their freedom only within the element for which they have been created.

We come now to human beings. If fish were made for water, what were human beings made for? The biblical answer surely is that if fish were made for water, human beings were made for love, for loving God and loving our neighbour. Love is the element in which humans find their distinctive humanness. As Robert Southwell, the sixteenth-century Roman Catholic poet wrote, 'not where I breathe, but where I love, I live'. He was consciously echoing Augustine's epigram that the soul lives when it

loves, not when it exists. An authentically human existence is impossible without love.

This brings us to a startling human paradox. Let me
state it simply like this: true freedom is freedom to be my
true self, as God made me and meant me to be. But God
made me for loving, and loving is giving, self-giving.
Therefore, in order to be myself, I have to deny myself,
and give myself in love for God and others. In order to be
free, I have to serve. In order to live, I have to die to
my own self-centredness. In
order to find myself I have
to lose myself in loving. I
have read somewhere that
Michelangelo put it beautifully in these words: 'When I
am yours, then at last I am
completely myself.' For I am
not myself until I am yours
(God's and others').

*'When I am
yours, then at
last I am
completely myself.'*

So freedom is the exact
opposite of what most people think it is. I remember a
Finnish student at the University of Helsinki, who said to
me: 'If only I could be free of responsibility to God and
other people, then I could live for myself. Then I would
be free.' But true freedom is the opposite. It is liberation
from a preoccupation with my silly little self in order to be
free to love God and my neighbour.

Jesus himself taught this fundamental paradox of
freedom. According to the Authorized Version, he said:

'Whosoever will save his life shall lose it; but whosoever shall lose his life for my sake and the gospel's, the same shall save it' (Mark 8:35). I used to think that he was referring to martyrs, and to the literal, physical saving and losing of lives. But the Greek noun the AV translates 'life' is *psychē*, which in many contexts is best rendered 'self'. Or it may take the place of a simple reflexive pronoun, 'yourself'. In modern English one might translate Jesus' epigram like this:

> 'If you insist on holding on to yourself and living for yourself and refusing to let yourself go, you will lose yourself. But if you are prepared to lose yourself, to give yourself away in love for God and your fellow human beings, then in that moment of complete abandon, when you think you have lost everything, the miracle takes place and you find yourself.'

Christ is the key to freedom, and this is the fifth reason why I am a Christian.

I have come that they may have life, and have it to the full.

JOHN 10:10

Chapter 6

THE FULFILMENT OF OUR ASPIRATIONS

The sixth reason why I am a Christian can be simply stated. It is this: all human beings have a number of basic aspirations or longings, which (I am persuaded) only Jesus Christ can fulfil. This is not just a theory; it is a claim validated by millions of Christians, among whom I think and hope I could include myself. There is a hunger in the human heart which none but Christ can satisfy. There is a thirst which none but he can quench. There is an inner emptiness which none but he can fill. As Augustine wrote at the very beginning of his *Confessions*, 'You have made us for yourself, and our heart is restless until it rests in you.'[1]

But, as we investigate this claim, two immediate objections are likely to be raised. The first is that Jesus Christ is evidently a crutch. 'He's fine', people say, 'for lame dogs who need a helping hand, but for able-bodied, strong-minded people who can manage on their own, he is entirely superfluous.'

I begin my response by agreeing with the criticism. Jesus Christ is indeed a crutch for the lame, to help us walk upright, just as he is also medicine for the spiritually sick, bread for the hungry and water for the thirsty. We do not deny this; it is perfectly true. But then all human beings are lame, sick, hungry and thirsty. The only difference between us is not that some are needy, while others are not. It is rather that some know and acknowledge their need, while others either don't through ignorance or won't through pride.

The second objection that is sometimes raised is that Jesus Christ is evidently a fiction of our own mind. Some people put it like this: 'The belief that Jesus Christ meets our human needs gives the game away. He's nothing more than a figment of your imagination. You feel unloved and unwanted; so you create your own heavenly father figure. You feel spiritually hungry; so you invent Jesus Christ as the bread of life.'

My response to this second objection is that the argument lacks logic. Does the fact that food satisfies our physical hunger make us suspicious of food? Does the fact that love brings us a sense of well-being rouse our suspicions about love? Then why should the fact that Christ fulfils our human aspirations rouse our suspicions about Christ? No, the correspondence between our aspirations and their fulfilment in Christ is due not to a fantasy of our own minds, but to a reality that God has established. C. S. Lewis put it with his customary clarity: 'Our life-long nostalgia, our longing to be reunited with something in the universe from which we now feel cut off, our desire to be on the inside of a door which we have always seen from the outside: this is no mere neurotic fancy, but the truest index of our real situation.'[2]

Having considered the two commonest objections which people raise to our claim that Christ fulfils our human aspirations, we are ready to look more deeply into the claim itself. And this leads us to the second chapter of Paul's letter to the Colossians: 'For in Christ all the fulness of the Deity lives in bodily form' (verse 9); 'and you have been given fulness in Christ' (verse 10).

To be a Christian is to be truly and fully human.

Common to both these astonishing statements (the first about Christ, the second about us) are the word 'fulness' and the expression 'in Christ'. In Christ God's fulness dwells permanently, and in Christ (united to him) we ourselves have come to fulness of life. Everything essential to the divine being is in Christ, and everything essential to our human being is in us if we are in Christ. To be a Christian, then, is not to be an oddity, condemned to perpetual eccentricity; it is rather to be truly and fully human, to have come to 'fulness'. Conversely, to reject Christ is to become to some degree subhuman, because it is to forfeit experiences indispensable to authentic humanness.

What, then, are these experiences, these human longings? My thesis is that human beings have three basic aspirations that only Jesus Christ can fulfil.

1. THE QUEST FOR TRANSCENDENCE

'Transcendence', until fairly recently, has been a rather pedantic word, little used and little understood, largely restricted to institutions of theological learning, which distinguish between 'transcendence' (meaning 'God above us') and 'immanence' (meaning 'God with and among us'). Nowadays, however, particularly because of the craze for transcendental meditation, everybody has some idea what transcendence means. The quest for transcendence is the search for a Reality that is above and beyond the material order. It arises from the conviction that Reality cannot be confined to a test tube or smeared on a slide and subjected to microscopic examination. There is something else, something more, something awesome, which no scientific instrument is able to apprehend or measure.

One author who has given eloquent expression to this contemporary loss of the transcendent is Theodore Roszak, whose statements are all the more striking because he is not a professing Christian. His best-known book, following *The Making of a Counter Culture* (1968), is probably *Where the Wasteland Ends* (1972), which is intriguingly subtitled 'Politics and Transcendence in a Post-Industrial Society'. He bemoans what he calls the 'coca-colonization of the world'.[3] We are suffering today, he says, from 'a psychic claustrophobia within the scientific worldview',[4] in which the human spirit cannot breathe. Roszak goes on to castigate science (I think he means pseudo-science) for its reductionist assault on human life and its arrogant claim to be able to explain everything. He speaks of its 'debunking spirit'[5] and its 'undoing of the mysteries'.[6] The materialistic world of objective science is not nearly 'spacious enough' for the human spirit.[7] Without transcendence 'the person shrivels'.[8]

Whether Roszak realized it or not, he was only echoing Jesus who, quoting Deuteronomy, said that human beings do 'not live on bread alone' (Deuteronomy 8:3; Matthew 4:4). In other words, we are more than material bodies needing food; we are spiritual beings needing God, needing transcendence.

Several other examples could be given of this disillusion with secularism and this loss of transcendence. The distinguished sociologist Peter Berger has offered the 'simple hypothesis' that the current occult wave 'is to be understood as resulting from the repression of transcendence in modern consciousness'.[9] Richard North, former environment correspondent of *The Independent*, confessed that 'an awful lot of us just need to worship something ... we are all falling in love with the environment as an extension to and in lieu of having fallen out of love with God'.[10] More surprising still is A. N. Wilson. Although he affirms that he has now 'discarded any formal religious allegiance', which he dismisses as 'that moribund combination of superstition and deceit', he nevertheless acknowledges that he still has 'strong religious impulses within himself', and that he experiences 'feelings of nameless humility before the mystery of things'.[11]

Yet more striking than these individual confessions is the overthrow of Marxism. Trevor Beeson has written that 'the basic doctrines of Communism have neither convinced the minds, nor satisfied the emotions, of the intelligentsia or of the proletariat'.[12] What Solzhenitsyn called the 'Communist steamroller'[13] was unable to crush the human spirit and its quest for transcendence.

So wherever transcendence has been lost, people are longing for its recovery. They seek it through mind-expanding drugs and the so-called 'higher consciousness', through the speculative fantasies of science fiction, through music and the other arts, through sex (which Malcolm Muggeridge used to call 'the mysticism of the materialist'), through yoga and other expressions of eastern religion.

Most remarkable of all recent religious trends is perhaps the rise of the New Age movement in the West. It is a bizarre assortment of diverse beliefs, including religion and science, physics and metaphysics, ancient pantheism and evolutionary optimism, astrology, spiritism, reincarnation, ecology and alternative medicine. David Spangler, one of the movement's leaders, is the author of *Emergence: The Rebirth of the Sacred*.[14] In it he writes that 'from a very early age' he had himself been 'aware of an extra dimension' to the world around him, which, as he grew older, he came to identify as 'a sacred or transcendental dimension'. 'The rebirth of the sense of the sacred', he says, 'is at the heart of the new age.'[15]

Our Christian reaction to the New Age phenomenon, and to every other expression of the quest for transcendence, should (it seems to me) be one of understanding. For we should be able to grasp what is happening. When the apostle Paul stood before the philosophers in Athens and responded to the extreme religiosity of its citizens, he described them as reaching out for God (Acts 17:27), groping for their Creator in the darkness.

Christians believe, moreover, that this is a fundamental human aspiration that only Jesus Christ can fulfil for, though sin alienates us from God, Christ died for our sins in order to reconcile us to God (1 Peter 3:18). And, once reconciled to God through Christ, everything changes. We walk each day with God. We live in his presence. It becomes natural to listen to his voice as he speaks to us through the Bible, and it becomes equally natural to speak to him in prayer. For basic to our Christian discipleship is the cultivation of a personal relationship with God. God becomes the great reality of our lives.

Then, on the Lord's Day (as the New Testament calls Sunday), together we bow down before him in that mixture of awe, love, wonder and joy that we call worship. For as we come to meet him, he comes to meet us. In fulfilment of the promise of Jesus, that whenever even only two or three have met in his name, he is there among them

(Matthew 18:20). He also makes himself known to us both through his Word (as it is read and expounded) and through Holy Communion (the bread and wine dramatizing visibly the promise of his forgiveness). Indeed, Christian public worship is the peak and pinnacle of Christian experience. Not always, of course. Sometimes church services are ritual without reality. But Jesus condemned this kind of formalism. Quoting Isaiah the prophet (29:13) he said: 'These people honour me with their lips, but their hearts are far from me' (Mark 7:6). But when worship is real, our hearts and minds are transported beyond time and space to join the whole church on earth and in heaven in the worship of God. Then we know what Jacob meant when he said, 'Surely the LORD is in this place', and sometimes unbelievers coming in will fall down and worship with us, saying, 'God is really among you!' (Genesis 28:16; 1 Corinthians 14:24–25).

When worship is real, our hearts and minds are transported beyond time and space to join the whole church on earth and in heaven in the worship of God.

To me it is a great tragedy that many modern men and women who are seeking transcendence turn to drugs, sex, yoga, cults and the New Age instead of to Christ and his church, in whose worship services true transcendence should always be experienced, and a close encounter with the living God enjoyed.

2. THE QUEST FOR SIGNIFICANCE

There is much in contemporary society that not only smothers our sense of transcendence but also diminishes (and even destroys) our sense of personal significance, our belief that life has any meaning. Three tendencies may be mentioned.

First, there is the effect of *technology*. Technology can be liberating, of course, in so far as it frees people from domestic or industrial drudgery. But it can also be dreadfully dehumanizing, as men and women feel themselves to be no longer persons but things, 'identified not by a "proper name" but by a serial number punched on a card [or, as we would say, converted into a barcode] that has been designed to travel through the entrails of a computer'.[16]

Secondly, there is *scientific reductionism*. Some scientists from different disciplines have argued that a human being is nothing but an animal (Desmond Morris's 'naked ape', to be precise), or nothing but a machine, programmed to make automatic responses to external stimuli. It was statements like these that prompted the late Professor Donald MacKay to popularize the expression 'nothing buttery' as an explanation of what is meant by 'reductionism', and to protest against every tendency to reduce human beings to a level lower than the fully personal.

To be sure, our brain is a machine, a highly complex mechanism. And our anatomy and physiology are those of an animal. But this is not a complete account of our humanness. There is more to us than a body and a brain. It is when people affirm that we are 'nothing but' this or that, that they make a serious and dangerous mistake.

Thirdly, *existentialism* has the effect of diminishing people's sense of significance. Radical existentialists may be said to differ from humanists in general by their resolve to take their atheism seriously and to face its terrible consequences. As we saw in chapter 4, because (in their view) God is dead, everything else has died with him. Because there is no God, there are no values or ideals either, no moral laws or standards, no purposes or meanings. And, although I exist, there is yet nothing that gives me or my existence any significance, except perhaps my decision to seek the courage to be. Meaning is found only in despising my own meaninglessness. There is no other way to authenticate myself.

Significance is basic to survival.

Bleakly heroic as this philosophy may sound, there must be very few people able to perform the conjuring trick of pretending to have significance when they know they have none. For significance is basic to survival.

This is what Viktor Frankl found when, as a young

man, he spent three years in the Auschwitz concentration camp. He noticed that the inmates most likely to survive their ordeal were those 'who knew that there was a task waiting for them to fulfil'.[17] He quotes Nietzsche's assertion that 'he who has a *why* to live for can bear almost any *how*'.[18]

Later Frankl became Professor of Psychiatry and Neurology in the University of Vienna and founded the so-called 'Third Viennese School of Psychiatry'. He postulated that, in addition to Freud's 'will to pleasure' and Adler's 'will to power', human beings have a 'will to meaning'.[19] Indeed, 'the striving to find a meaning in one's life is the primary motivational force in man'.[20]

So he developed what he called 'logotherapy', using *logos* to mean neither 'word' nor 'reason' but 'meaning'. 'The mass neurosis of the present time', he wrote, is 'the existential vacuum',[21] that is, the loss of a sense that life is meaningful. He would sometimes ask his patients, 'Why don't you commit suicide?' (an extraordinary question for a doctor to ask!). They would reply that there was something (perhaps their work, marriage or family) that made their life worthwhile for them. Professor Frankl would then build on this.

Meaninglessness leads to boredom, alcoholism, juvenile delinquency and suicide. Commenting on Viktor Frankl's work, Arthur Koestler wrote:

> It is an inherent tendency in man to reach out for *meanings* to fulfil and for *values* to actualize ... Thousands and thousands

of young students are exposed to an indoctrination ... which denies the existence of values. The result is a world-wide phenomenon – more and more patients are crowding our clinics with the complaint of an inner emptiness, the sense of a total and ultimate meaninglessness of life.[22]

According to Emile Durkheim, in his classic study of suicide, the greatest number of suicides are caused by *anomie*, which could be rendered 'normlessness' or 'meaninglessness'. And 'anomic' suicide takes place when somebody either has no goal in life or pursues an unattainable goal, whether power, success or prestige. 'No human being can be happy or even exist unless his needs are sufficiently proportioned to his means.'[23]

Now I venture to claim that Jesus Christ can fulfil this second basic human aspiration. He gives us a sense of personal significance, because he tells us who we are. To begin with, he took over from the Old Testament that great affirmation that we have already considered

> God created man
>   in his own image,
> in the image of God
>   he created him;
> male and female
>   he created them.
> (Genesis 1:27)

That is to say, as we saw in chapter 4, the Creator endowed us with a cluster of rational, moral, social and spiritual faculties that make us like God and unlike the animals. Human beings are God-like beings and the divine image in us, although it has been marred, has not been destroyed. Hence Jesus spoke of our value. He said that we were of much more value than a sheep (Matthew 12:12) or than many sparrows (Matthew 10:31; Luke 12:24).

He not only taught it; he exhibited it. His whole mission demonstrated the value he placed on people. He treated everybody with respect – women and men, children and adults, the sinner and the righteous. For he was the good shepherd, he said, who missed only one lost sheep and risked danger and death to find it. So he went to the cross, deliberately and voluntarily, to lay down his life for his sheep. Nothing can convince us of our personal significance like the cross of Christ. As Archbishop William Temple put it, 'my worth is what I am worth to God, and that is a marvellous great deal, for Christ died for me'.[24]

Christian teaching on the dignity and worth of human beings is of the utmost importance today, not only for our own self-image and self-respect, but also for the welfare of society. When human beings are devalued, everything in society tends to turn sour. There is no freedom, no dignity, no carefree joy. Human life seems not worth living, because it is scarcely human any longer. But when human beings are valued as persons, because of their intrinsic worth, everything changes. Why? Because people matter. Because every man, woman and child has worth and significance as a human being made in God's image and likeness.

3. THE QUEST FOR COMMUNITY

The technocratic society, which diminishes and even destroys transcendence and significance, is destructive of human community as well. Ours is an era of social disintegration, especially in the West. People find it increasingly difficult to relate to one another or to find love in a loveless world. I choose three very different people as witnesses to this.

Every man, woman and child has worth and significance as a human being made in God's image and likeness.

It seems appropriate to begin with Bertrand Russell, since his rejection of Christianity was the springboard for this book. In the Prologue to his autobiography he wrote with moving candour:

Three passions, simple but overwhelmingly strong, have governed my life: the longing for love, the search for knowledge, and unbearable pity for the suffering of mankind. These passions, like great winds, have blown me hither and thither, in a wayward course, over a deep ocean of anguish, reaching to the very verge of despair. I have sought love, first, because it brings ecstasy ... I have sought it, next, because it relieves loneliness –

that terrible loneliness in which one's shivering consciousness looks over the rim of the world into the cold unfathomable life-less abyss ...[25]

My second witness is Mother Teresa. Born in Yugoslavia of Albanian parents, she left for India when she was only seventeen years old. Then in 1948, after about twenty years of teaching, she gave up this profession in order to serve the poorest of the poor in Calcutta, and became an Indian citizen. So India was her home for well over sixty years, and her voice and vision were those of the Third World. This is what she wrote about the West:

'People today are hungry for love.'

People today are hungry for love, for understanding love, which is ... the only answer to loneliness and great poverty. That is why we [sc. the sisters and brothers of her order] are able to go to countries like England and America and Australia, where there is no hunger for bread. But there people are suffering from terrible loneliness, terrible despair, terrible hatred, feeling unwanted, feeling helpless, feeling hopeless. They have forgotten how to smile, they have forgotten the beauty of the human touch. They are forgetting what is human love ...[26]

I remember that, when I first read this assessment of the western world, I was a bit indignant and considered it exaggerated. But I have since changed my mind. I think it is accurate, at least as a generalization.

Woody Allen is my third witness. For all his acclaimed brilliance as an author, director and actor, he seems never to have found either himself or anybody else. In his film *Manhattan* (1979) he quips that he thinks people ought to 'mate for life, like pigeons or Catholics', but he appears unable to follow his own precept. He confesses that all his films 'deal with that greatest of all difficulties – love relationships. Everybody encounters that. People are either in love, about to fall in love, on the way out of love, looking for love or a way to avoid it'.[27] His biographer ends his portrait of him with these words: 'He is struggling, as *we* are surely struggling, to find the strength to found a life upon a love. As the character says in *Hannah and Her Sisters*, "Maybe the poets are right. Maybe love is the only answer …"'[28]

Here then are three people of very different backgrounds, beliefs, temperaments and experiences, who nevertheless agree about the paramount importance of love. They speak for the human race. We all know instinctively that love is indispensable to our humanness. Love is what life is all about.

So people are seeking it everywhere. At least since the 1960s, some have been breaking away from western individualism and experimenting with communal styles of living. Others are trying to replace the nuclear family (typical in the West) with the extended family (traditional for centuries in Asia and Africa). Yet others are repudiating the age-long institutions of marriage and family in an attempt (vain and foolish, Christians believe) to find in this way the freedom and spontaneity of love. Everybody seems to be searching for genuine community and the authentic relationships of love. For 'love, love changes everything', as Andrew Lloyd Webber's lyric runs in *Aspects of Love*.

And our sincere Christian claim is that only Jesus Christ can fulfil this third basic human aspiration, for love. To be sure, I am not suggesting that love is absent outside the Christian community, since, there too, love binds parents and children, brothers and sisters, husband and wife. But there is a yet deeper dimension of love that flows from Christ. As the apostle John wrote in his first letter: 'this is how we know what love is: Jesus Christ laid down his life for us'. Again, 'this is love: not that we loved God, but that he loved us' (1 John 3:16; 4:10).

And although, alas! there are many Christian communities and fellowships that fall far short of the divine ideal, there are others that beautifully approximate to it. They enable us to affirm that God's purpose is not just to save isolated individuals, and so perpetuate our loneliness, but rather to build a new society, a new family, even a new human race, that lives a new life and a new lifestyle. Bishop Stephen Neill expressed this well:

> Within the fellowship of those who are bound together by personal loyalty to Jesus Christ, the relationship of love reaches an

intimacy and intensity unknown elsewhere. Friendship between the friends of Jesus of Nazareth is unlike any other
friendship. This ought to be normal experience within the
Christian community ... where it is experienced, especially
across the barriers of race, nationality and language, it is one of
the most convincing evidences of the continuing activity of
Jesus among men.[29]

God's purpose is to build a new society, a new family, even a new human race, that lives a new life and a new lifestyle.

Here, then, is the threefold quest on which all human beings are engaged. Although they may not articulate it in this way, I think we may say that in looking for transcendence they are seeking God, in looking for significance they are seeking themselves, and in looking for community they are seeking their neighbour. For this is humankind's universal search – for God, for neighbour and for ourselves.

Moreover, it is our Christian claim (confident I know, humble I hope) that those who seek will find – in Christ and in his new community. For he died to reconcile us to God; he demonstrated through his life and death our fundamental worth; and he introduces us into his new society.

That he thus fulfils our human aspirations, and so brings us to fulness of life, is a further reason why I am a Christian.

Come to me, all you who are weary and burdened,

and I will give you rest.

Take my yoke upon you and learn from me,

for I am gentle and humble in heart,

and you will find rest for your souls.

For my yoke is easy and my burden is light.

MATTHEW 11:28–30

Chapter 7

THE GREATEST OF ALL INVITATIONS

·

We all like receiving invitations, whether to a meal, a party, a concert or a wedding. Usually at the bottom of the invitation card those cryptic letters are printed: RSVP, and those of us who have been brought up in a western culture know what they stand for, namely a polite request in French to respond to the invitation (*Répondez s'il vous plait*).

Not everybody knows this, however. I think of a married couple who had fled from Eastern Europe before the Second World War and found asylum in the UK. Their knowledge of western culture was distinctly limited. So when they received an invitation to a wedding, which concluded with RSVP, they were flummoxed. 'Vife,' said the husband, in his thick, eastern accent, 'vot does it mean, RSVP? I do not know vot it means.' Then suddenly, after prolonged reflection, inspiration dawned. 'Vife,' said the husband, 'I know vot it means: Remember Send Vedding Present!'

That couple thought the card was a demand, when in reality it was an invitation. Many people make the same mistake today about Jesus Christ and the gospel. They miss the fact that it is a free invitation, indeed the greatest invitation anyone ever receives. Here is its essence: 'Come to me, all you who are weary and burdened, and I will give you rest' (Matthew 11:28).

These words must surely be among the most appealing that Jesus ever spoke. It is no wonder that the crowds 'listened to him with delight', and 'were amazed at the gracious words that came from his lips' (Mark 12:37; Luke 4:22). The invitation of Jesus to come to him has been immortalized by musicians, liturgists and artists. Thus Handel, in one of the best-known arias of *Messiah*, skilfully combined Jesus' words with words from Isaiah: 'He shall feed his flock like a shepherd; come unto him.' Then in the sixteenth century Thomas Cranmer took Jesus' invitation from the German liturgy of Archbishop Hermann of Cologne and incorporated it in his reformed prayer book, so that every time Anglican worshippers attend a Communion Service according to the 1662 Prayer Book they are invited to listen to the 'comfortable words our Saviour Christ saith unto all that truly turn to him', namely, 'Come unto me all that travail and are heavy laden, and I will refresh you.' One more example comes from the early twentieth-century religious artist and Bible illustrator Harold Copping. He painted Jesus on a hillside with large crowds gathered below him. Jesus' arms are stretched out in welcome, and underneath is written the simple caption, 'Come unto me.'

In 1996, as a seventy-fifth birthday present from friends, I had the good fortune to visit South Georgia Island in the South Atlantic, some 800 miles east of the Falkland Islands. We landed at Grytviken, an abandoned Norwegian whaling station, where the great British explorer Ernest Shackleton is buried. Nearby is a tiny Lutheran church, recently restored, and now surrounded by king penguins and elephant seals. The church door responded to my touch, and what do you think I found? On the church's east wall are inscribed in Norwegian the same invitation of Jesus: 'Come to me, all you who are weary and burdened, and I will give you rest.'

This appeal ('Come to me') is the most famous part of the passage. It is, however, embedded in a paragraph of six verses, which need to be kept together. They contain two invitations addressed to us, preceded by two affirmations that Jesus made about himself. And we are not in a position to respond to the invitations until we have considered and accepted the affirmations. Jesus said:

'I praise you, Father, Lord of heaven and earth, because you have hidden these things from the wise and learned, and revealed them to little children. Yes, Father, for this was your good pleasure.

'All things have been committed to me by my Father. No-one knows the Son except the Father, and no-one knows the Father except the Son and those to whom the Son chooses to reveal him.

'Come to me, all you who are weary and burdened, and I will give you rest. Take my yoke upon you and learn from me, for I am gentle and humble in heart, and you will find rest for your souls. For my yoke is easy and my burden is light' (Matthew 11:25–30).

1. TWO AFFIRMATIONS

The two affirmations both concern that most important of all subjects, the knowledge of God. Is it possible for human beings to come to know God, for creatures to know their Creator? And if so, how is it possible for us to do so? Jesus addresses himself to these questions when he says that the Father has 'hidden these things from the wise and learned, and revealed them to little children' and that 'no-one knows the Father except the Son and those to whom the Son chooses to reveal him'. We note at once that the word common to both affirmations is the verb 'revealed'. The implication is that there can be no knowledge of God without his initiative in revelation.

First, *God is revealed only by Jesus Christ.* It may be helpful to jump straight to the second statement of verse 27: 'No-one knows the Father except the Son and those to whom the Son chooses to reveal him.' That is to say, only Jesus knows God, so only he can make him known. This means, of course, that God is fully and finally revealed in

Jesus Christ. It does not deny that there are other and lesser revelations. For example, God is partially revealed in the ordered loveliness of the created universe, in the moral demands of the human conscience and in the unfolding developments of history. But, although creation speaks of God's glory, conscience of his righteousness, and history of his providence and power, nobody tells us of his love for human beings in their alienation and lostness, or of his plan to rescue us and reconcile us to himself, except Jesus of Nazareth.

This is the claim of Jesus, as we have already seen. And this is why every enquiry into the truth of Christianity must begin with the historic person of Jesus. The most unnerving thing about him is the quiet, unassuming yet confident way in which he advanced his stupendous claims. There was no fanfare of trumpets, no boasting and no ostentation. His manner was altogether unaffected. Yet here he is daring to call 'the Lord of heaven and earth' (the creator and sustainer of all things) his Father, and himself the Father's Son (verse 25), indeed 'the Son' in an absolute way; and that all things have been committed to him by his Father (that is, that he is the heir of the universe). And finally he claims that as only he knows the Father, so only

Every enquiry into the truth of Christianity must begin with the historic person of Jesus.

the Father knows him; he is an enigma to all others. There therefore exists between them an unparalleled reciprocal relationship. This is Jesus' multiple claim. It is breathtaking in its sweep. Nobody else has dared to make it, while retaining his moral integrity, sanity and balance.

Jesus' second affirmation is that *God is revealed only to babies.* Verses 25–26: 'At that time Jesus said, "I praise you, Father, Lord of heaven and earth, because you have hidden these things from the wise and learned, and revealed them to little children [*nēpioi,* babies]. Yes, Father, for this was your good pleasure."'

By 'babies' Jesus meant not those who are young in years but those who (whatever their age) are humble and childlike. 'Babies' in the vocabulary of Jesus are sincere and humble seekers; from everybody else, Jesus said, God actively hides himself.

Please do not misunderstand this. This is not obscurantism. It is not to copy the ostrich and bury our head in the sand. It is not to murder our intellect or deny the importance of thought, for we have been told to 'stop thinking like children' and instead in our thinking to be adults (1 Corinthians 14:20).

No. It is simply to acknowledge the limitations of the human mind. When seeking God it flounders helplessly out of its depth. For by definition God is infinite in his being, whereas our little, finite mind, capable as it is of remarkable achievements in the empirical sciences, is utterly incapable of discovering God.

If, then, we stand on our proud pedestal, with our

spectacles on our nose, presuming to scrutinize and crit-
icize God, and proclaiming the autonomy of our own
reason, we will never find him. It is not only unseemly to
treat God like that; it is also unproductive. For according
to Jesus God actively hides himself from people like that.

If, however, we step down from our lofty platform and
humble ourselves before God; if we confess our inability to
find him by ourselves; if we
get down reverently on our
knees and read the story of
Jesus in the Gospels with the
open mind of a little child,
God reveals himself to such.
Is this perhaps why some of
my readers have not yet
found God? Is it that you
have sought him in the wrong
mood? What is required of us
is not that we close our
minds, but that we open
them; not that we stifle them,
but that we humble them.

*What is required
of us is not that
we close our
minds, but that
we open them; not
that we stifle
them, but that we
humble them.*

So far we have reflected on Jesus' two affirmations concerning the knowledge of God. It is as if we have been
given answers to two fundamental questions. Firstly, who
can reveal God? Answer: only Jesus Christ. Secondly, to
whom does God reveal himself? Answer: only to 'babies'.
God hides himself from intellectual dilettantes, but reveals
himself in Christ to those who humbly seek him.

2. TWO INVITATIONS

We turn now from the two affirmations that Jesus made to the two invitations he issued and continues to issue today. Here is the first: 'Come to me, all you who are weary and burdened, and I will give you rest' (Matthew 11:28). This invitation is addressed to all human beings, including us. In issuing it, Jesus is being far from complimentary. He describes us as 'weary and burdened' or 'labouring and heavy laden'. He seems to be likening us to oxen, labouring under a yoke that chafes on our neck, and bearing a heavy, even a crushing, load.

Thus Jesus assumes that all human beings are burdened, and I for one do not doubt the accuracy of his diagnosis. There are the burdens of our anxieties and our fears, our temptations, our responsibilities and our loneliness. There is the terrible sense, which sometimes engulfs us, that life has neither meaning nor purpose. Above all, there is the burden of our failures or (to give them their proper name) our sins, which deserve God's judgment. Does our conscience never feel its guilt? Is our head never bowed down with a sense of shame and alienation? Have we never cried out, as the Anglican Prayer Book obliges us to, that 'the burden of our sins is intolerable' (that is, we can bear it no longer)?

If not, if we are strangers to all this heaviness, I fear that we shall never accept Christ's invitation to come to him for release. It is the burdened to whom he promises rest. As he said elsewhere, 'it is not the healthy who need a doctor, but the sick' (Matthew 9:12). In other words, just as we don't go to the doctor unless we are ill, so we shall not come to Jesus Christ unless and until we acknowledge the burden of our sin. The very first step to becoming a follower of Jesus Christ is the humble admission that we need him. Nothing keeps us out of the kingdom of God more surely than our pride and self-sufficiency.

Having considered to whom Jesus addresses his invitation, we are in a position to consider what it is that he offers us. He promises, if we come to him, to ease our yoke, to lift our burden, to set us free, to give us rest.

Nothing keeps us out of the kingdom of God more surely than our pride and self-sufficiency.

Some years ago I visited a student group in Cuba, in which there was widespread disillusion over the failed experiment of Marxism. One male student described his experience. He had been a Christian for only four months, he said. Previously, like everybody else in Cuba, he had felt overloaded with shortages and poverty, by existential emptiness and alienation, until he asked Jesus Christ to give him peace and tranquillity and to free him from his burdens. He received such relief from the promise of Matthew 11:28 that he could hardly sleep. The next day he perceived himself to be different. No medicine had been able to give him tranquillity; he was still poor, but Jesus Christ had given him rest.

And only Jesus Christ can do these things. For he is portrayed in the New Testament as the world's supreme burden-bearer, since he bore our burden on the cross. Listen again to these well-known words from the Bible:

> The LORD has laid on him
>   the iniquity of us all.
> (Isaiah 53:6)

> For he bore the sin of many (Isaiah 53:12).

> 'Look, the Lamb of God, who takes away the sin of the world!' (John 1:29).

> He himself bore our sins in his body on the tree (1 Peter 2:24).

> Christ was sacrificed once to take away the sins of many people (Hebrews 9:28).

These verses all speak of Jesus Christ as 'bearing' our sins and so taking them away. To 'bear sin' is a frequent Old Testament expression for bearing the penalty of sin. The penalty is paid either by the sinner or by the God-given substitute. This is the very essence of the gospel.

The good news, then, is this: that Almighty God loves us in spite of our rebellion against him; that he came after us himself in the person of his Son Jesus Christ; that he took our nature and became a human being; that he lived a perfect life of love, having no sins of his own for which atonement needed to be made, but that on the cross he identified himself with our sin and guilt. In two dramatic New Testament expressions he was 'made ... to be sin for us' and became 'a curse for us' (2 Corinthians 5:21; Galatians 3:13). For in those awful three hours of God-forsaken darkness he endured the condemnation our sins had deserved. But now, on the ground of Christ's sin-bearing death, God offers us a full and free forgiveness, together with a new birth and a new beginning in the power of his resurrection.

Nobody has described more dramatically than John Bunyan in *The Pilgrim's Progress* the exhilaration of losing the burden of our sin.

Up this way therefore did burdened Christian run, but not without great difficulty, because of the load on his back.

He ran thus till he came at a place somewhat ascending; and upon that place stood a Cross, and a little below, in the bottom, a Sepulchre. So I saw in my dream, that just as Christian came up with the Cross, his burden loosed from off his shoulders, and fell from off his back, and began to tumble, and so continued to do, till it came to the mouth of the Sepulchre, where it fell in, and I saw it no more.

Then was Christian glad and lightsome, and said, with a merry heart, He hath given me rest by His sorrow, and life by His death. Then he stood still awhile to look and wonder, for it was very surprising to him, that the sight of the Cross should thus ease him of his burden. He looked therefore, and looked again, even till the springs that were in his head sent the waters down his cheeks ... Now, as he stood looking and weeping, behold, three Shining Ones came to him and saluted him with 'Peace be to thee.' So the first said to him, 'Thy sins be forgiven thee' ...; the second stripped him of his rags, and clothed him with change of raiment; the third also set a mark on his forehead, and gave him a roll with a seal upon it ... that he should give it in at the Celestial Gate ...

Then Christian gave three leaps for joy, and went on singing:

> 'Thus far did I come laden with my sin,
> Nor could aught ease the grief that I was in,
> Till I came hither. What a place is this!
> Must here be the beginning of my bliss?
> Must here the burden fall from off my back?
> Must here the strings that bound it to me crack?
> Blest Cross! blest Sepulchre! blest, rather, be
> The Man that there was put to shame for me!'[1]

Salvation is a gift that is absolutely free and utterly undeserved.

Having considered the questions to whom the invitation of Jesus is addressed, and what he offers, the third question concerns what he asks from us. The plain answer is 'Nothing!' – except that we come to him. For he has done everything else. Salvation is a gift that is absolutely free and utterly undeserved.

Yet there is no substitute for this personal coming to Jesus Christ. Some people become engrossed in the externals of religion. They come to church. They come to be baptized and confirmed. They come to a pastor to seek his counsel. They come to the Bible and read it, together with other religious literature. But it is possible to engage in all these 'comings' without ever coming to Jesus Christ himself. I beg you not to stumble over the simplicity of Christ's invitation.

There was a famous Professor of Hebrew at Edinburgh University from 1843 to 1870. His name was Dr John Duncan, but because of his familiarity with Hebrew language and literature he was known affectionately to his students as 'Rabbi Duncan'. Such were his attainments in the Semitic languages that his students felt sure he said his prayers in Hebrew, and two of them determined to find out. They crept outside his bedroom door one night to listen. They expected to hear great flights of Hebrew rhetoric and mysticism. Instead, this is what they heard:

> Gentle Jesus, meek and mild,
> Look upon a little child;
> Pity my simplicity,
> Suffer me to come to thee.[2]

If a university professor could approach Jesus Christ like a child, I guess we can too. We may be sure that Rabbi Duncan did not encourage child*ish*ness in either himself or his students. But child-*like*ness is something quite different. For Jesus exalted the virtue of humility. He taught that, unless we humble ourselves like children, we shall not even enter God's kingdom (Matthew 18:1–3). He also taught, as we have seen, that God reveals himself only to 'babies', to humble seekers after the truth.[3]

If Jesus' first invitation is that we 'come' to him, his second is this: 'Take my yoke upon you and learn from me, for I am gentle and humble in heart, and you will find rest for your souls. For my yoke is easy and my burden is light' (Matthew 11:29–30).

I constantly marvel at the balance of the Bible. The Christian life is not just taking it easy and enjoying 'rest'. No; when we come to Jesus, a marvellous exchange takes place. He first eases our yoke and then fits his upon us instead. He first lifts our burden and then lays his upon us instead. But too many people, influenced by the 'pick 'n' mix' mentality of postmodernism, want the rest without the yoke; they want to lose their burden but not to gain Christ's. Yet the two invitations of Jesus belong together; we have no liberty to pick and choose between them.

What then is the 'yoke' of Christ? A yoke, of course, is a horizontal wooden bar which is laid on the necks of oxen when they are harnessed to a plough or a cart. And symbolically in Scripture it expresses submission to authority. Thus the Jews spoke of 'the yoke of Torah', because they submitted to the authority of God's law. Now, however, Jesus invites us to take his yoke upon us and – by doing so – to learn from him.

To take Christ's yoke upon us is to enter his school, to

become his disciples and to submit to his teaching authority. It implies that we are to regard him not only as our
saviour but also as our teacher and Lord. Jesus himself put
this beyond doubt when during his last night on earth he
said to the Twelve, 'You call me "Teacher" and "Lord", and
rightly so, for that is what I am' (John 13:13). In other
words, 'Teacher' and 'Lord' were more than courtesy titles;
they bore witness to a reality. It will include bringing every
part of our lives, public and private, under the sovereign
lordship of Jesus.

Does it sound hard? On the contrary, Jesus insists that it is the way of liber-ation. For the burden we lose when we come to Christ is heavy, whereas his burden, he said, is 'light'. Again, the yoke we lose when we come to Christ is a misfit; it chafes on our shoulders. But the

'You will know the truth, and the truth will set you free.'

yoke we gain is 'easy'; it is a perfect fit. 'My yoke is easy
and my burden is light.' How is this? I think it is that both
our mind and our will find their freedom under the
authority of Christ. The only authority under which our
mind is genuinely free is the authority of truth. So-called
'free thought', which claims licence to believe anything,
including lies, is not authentic intellectual freedom; it is
bondage to illusion and falsehood. As Jesus said elsewhere
to his disciples, 'you will know the truth, and the truth will

set you free' (John 8:32). Similarly, the only authority under which our will is truly free is the authority of righteousness as revealed in God's commandments. 'I will walk about in freedom', declared the psalmist, 'for I have sought out your precepts' (Psalm 119:45). And the reason freedom is found in obedience to God's commandments is that there is a fundamental correspondence between God's law and our moral nature. The requirements of his law are not alien to us, for they are the laws of our own human being, written by creation on our hearts (Romans 2:15).

Having described the compatibility of his yoke and his burden, Jesus goes on to describe himself. He is 'gentle and humble in heart', he says. What Jesus offers us is the light burden and easy yoke of a kind and gentle Master. Under them we find rest.

Dietrich Bonhoeffer knew about this. He was executed by the special order of Heinrich Himmler at the Flossenburg concentration camp in April 1945. He wrote in his book *The Cost of Discipleship* as follows:

> Only the man who follows the command of Jesus single-mindedly, and unresistingly lets his yoke rest upon him, finds his burden easy, and under its gentle pressure receives the power to persevere in the right way. The command of Jesus is hard, unutterably hard, for those who try to resist it. But for those who willingly submit the yoke is easy and the burden is light.[4]

CONCLUSION: RSVP

We have considered the two affirmations and the two invitations that Jesus made, and continues to make today. The affirmations are that only he can reveal God, and that he does so only to 'babies', while the two invitations are that we come to him and take upon us his yoke.

But have we noticed that, although the two invitations are different, the promise attached to them is precisely the same? To those who come to him he says, 'I will give you rest', and to those who assume his yoke he promises that 'you will find rest for your souls'.

It is under Christ's yoke that we find rest, and in his service that we find freedom.

Everybody is looking and longing for rest, for peace, for freedom. And Jesus tells us where it may be found – in losing our burden at the cross, and in submitting to his teaching authority. Freedom is indeed found in laying down our burden, but it is emphatically not found in discarding Christ's. We are back with the great paradox of Christian living. It is under Christ's yoke that we find rest, and in his service that we find freedom. It is when we lose ourselves that we find ourselves, and when we die to our self-centredness that we begin to live.

So why am I a Christian? It has become clear that there is no one overriding reason, but rather a cluster of interlocking reasons. Some have to do with Jesus Christ himself – his extraordinary claims for himself, which I cannot explain away; his sufferings and death, which throw light on the problem of pain; and his relentless pursuit of me, in which he would not let me go. Others are concerned more with me than with him: he helps me to understand myself in the paradox of my humanness and to find the fulfilment of my basic human aspirations. Yet another concerns the necessity of decision as he invites us to come to him for freedom and for rest.

To sum it up in a single sentence: he who claims to be both Son of God and saviour and judge of humankind now stands before us offering, if only we come to him, fulfilment, freedom and rest. Such an invitation from such a person cannot lightly be dismissed. He waits patiently for our response. RSVP!

It is many years ago that I made my response to Christ, kneeling at my bedside in a school dormitory. I have not regretted it. For I have experienced what Lord Reith (the first Director General of the BBC) once called 'the mystery and the magic of the indwelling Christ'.[5]

I wonder if you, my reader, are ready to take the same step? If so, perhaps you would find it helpful to get away and alone somewhere, and to echo this prayer, making it your own:

A PRAYER

Lord Jesus Christ,

I am aware that in different ways you have been seeking me.

I have heard you knocking at my door.

I believe –

that your claims are true;

that you died on the cross for my sins,

and that you have risen in triumph over death.

Thank you for your loving offer of forgiveness, freedom and fulfilment.

Now –

I turn from my sinful self-centredness.

I come to you as my Saviour.

I submit to you as my Lord.

Give me strength to follow you for the rest of my life. Amen.

NOTES

PREFACE

1. Bertrand Russell, ed. Paul Edwards, *Why I Am Not a Christian* (George Allen & Unwin, 1957).

2. John Stott, *The Contemporary Christian* (IVP, 1992).

1. THE HOUND OF HEAVEN

1. R. Moffat Gautrey, *This Tremendous Lover*, an exposition of Francis Thompson's 'The Hound of Heaven' (Epworth, 1932).

2. Francis Thompson, *The Hound of Heaven* (Burns, Oates & Washbourne Ltd, 1893), p. 9.

3. Gautrey, *This Tremendous Lover*, p. 29.

4. Ibid., p. 30.

5. Thompson, *The Hound of Heaven*, p.16.

6. Ibid., p. 17.

7. C. S. Lewis, *Surprised by Joy* (Geoffrey Bles, 1955; repr. Collins Fontana, 1981), p. 181. 'Legion' (meaning a unit of about 6,000 soldiers) was the name the Gadarene demoniac gave himself because he was conscious of being overpowered by a large number of evil spirits. See Mark 5:1–20.

8. Augustine, *Confessions*, a new translation by Henry Chadwick (OUP, 1992), Book 2.ii.

9. Ibid., Book 8.xii.

10. Ibid., Book 10.xxvii.

11. Malcolm Muggeridge, *Chronicles of Wasted Time*, Part I, *The Green Stick* (Collins, 1972), p. 125.

12. Malcolm Muggeridge, *Jesus Rediscovered* (Collins Fontana, 1969), pp. 32, 41.

13. See above, n. 7.

14. Lewis, *Surprised by Joy*, p. 169.

15. Ibid., pp. 181–182.

16. Ibid., pp. 179–180.

17. Ibid., p. 173.

18. Ibid., p. 170.

19. Ibid., pp. 182–183.

2. THE CLAIMS OF JESUS

1. Joachim Jeremias, *The Central Message of the New Testament* (SCM, 1965), pp. 16–17, 19–20, 21, 30.

2. Hugh Martin, *The Claims of Christ: A Study in His Self-portraiture* (SCM, 1955), pp. 42–43.

3. C. S. Lewis, *Mere Christianity* (Geoffrey Bles, 1952; revised edition Fount, 1997), p. 43.

3. THE CROSS OF CHRIST

1. Malcolm Muggeridge, *Jesus Rediscovered* (Collins Fontana, 1969), pp. 24–25.

2. Cicero, *Against Verres* II.64.165.

3. Cicero, *In Defence of Rabirius* V.16.467.

4. 'Le bon Dieu me pardonnera. C'est son métier.' Said to have been spoken by Heine on his deathbed, and quoted in James Denney, *The Death of Christ* (1902; Tyndale Press, 1951), p. 186.

5. Anselm, *Cur Deus Homo* i.xxi.

6. Carnegie Simpson, *The Fact of Christ* (Hodder & Stoughton, 1900), p. 109.

7. P. T. Forsyth, *The Justification of God* (Duckworth, 1916), p. 32.

4. THE PARADOX OF OUR HUMANNESS

1. Douglas Coupland, *Life after God* (Touchstone, 1994), p. 9.

2. Ibid., p. 304.

3. Keith Thomas, *Man and the Natural World: Changing Attitudes in England 1500–1800* (1983; Penguin, 1984), pp. 31–32, 37–39, 43, 166, 172.

4. J. S. Whale, *Christian Doctrine* (1941; Fontana, 1957), p. 33.

5. From *Mark Twain's Notebook* (1894).

6. J. S. Whale, *op. cit.*, p. 41.

7. William Shakespeare, *Hamlet*, Act II, scene 2.

8. Mark Twain, title of ch. 28 of *More Tramps Abroad* (Chatto & Windus, 1897).

9. Richard Holloway. Extract from a speech he gave at the Catholic Renewal Conference at Loughborough in April 1978.

10. Reinhold Niebuhr, *The Children of Light and the Children of Darkness: A Vindication of Democracy and a Critique of its Traditional Defenders* (Nisbet, 1945), p. vi.

11. Carl R. Rogers, *On Becoming a Person* (Constable, 1961), p. 87 and elsewhere.

5. THE KEY TO FREEDOM

1. John Fowles, *The Magus* (1966; revised edn Triad Panther, 1977), p. 10.

2. Graham McCann, *Woody Allen, New Yorker* (Polity, 1990), pp. 43, 84.

3. Ibid., pp. 43, 83.

4. Bertrand Russell, ed. Paul Edwards, *Why I Am Not a Christian* (George Allen & Unwin, 1957), p. 47.

5. Bertrand Russell, *A Free Man's Worship* (1902; University Paperbacks, 1976), pp. 10–17.

6. From 'I dye alive' by Robert Southwell, in D. H. S.

Nicholson and A. H. E. Lee (eds.), *The Oxford Book of English Mystical Verse* (Clarendon, 1917), p. 236.

6. THE FULFILMENT OF OUR ASPIRATIONS

1. Augustine, *Confessions*, a new translation by Henry Chadwick (OUP, 1992), Book I.i.

2. From C. S. Lewis's sermon 'The Weight of Glory', published in *Transposition and Other Addresses* (Geoffrey Bles, 1949), p. 30.

3. Theodore Roszak, *Where the Wasteland Ends* (Faber & Faber, 1972), p. 22.

4. Ibid., p. 66.

5. Ibid., pp. 227–228.

6. Ibid., p. 67.

7. Ibid., p. 70.

8. Ibid., p. xxi.

9. Peter L. Berger, *Facing up to Modernity* (1977; Penguin, 1979), p. 255.

10. Quoted by Jonathon Porritt and David Winner in *The Coming of the Greens* (Collins, 1988), pp. 251–252.

11. A. N. Wilson, *Against Religion* (Chatto Counterblast No. 19, 1991), pp. 3, 20, 44.

12. Trevor Beeson, *Discretion and Valour* (Collins, 1974), p. 24.

13. From his address on receiving the Templeton Prize in London in May 1983.

14. David Spangler, *The Rebirth of the Sacred* (Dell, 1984).

15. Ibid., pp. 12, 41.

16. Arnold Toynbee, quoted in *The Times* on 5 April 1969. See his *Experiences* (OUP, 1969).

17. Viktor E. Frankl, *Man's Search for Meaning*, originally published under the title *From Death-Camp to Existentialism* (1959; Washington Square Press, 1963), p. 165.

18. Ibid., p. 164.

19. Ibid., p. 154.

20. Ibid., p. 154.

21. Ibid., pp. 167, 204.

22. From the chapter 'Rebellion in Vacuum', which was Arthur Koestler's contribution to the symposium *Protest and Discontent*, ed. Bernard Crick and William Robson (Penguin, 1970), p. 22.

23. Emile Durkheim, *Suicide: A Study in Sociology* (1897; English translation 1952, Routledge & Kegan Paul, 1975), p. 246.

24. William Temple, *Citizen and Churchman* (Eyre & Spottiswoode, 1941), p. 74.

25. *The Autobiography of Bertrand Russell* (George Allen & Unwin, 1967), p. 13.

26. Desmond Doig, *Mother Teresa, Her People and Her Work* (Collins, 1976), p. 159.

27. Graham McCann, *Woody Allen, New Yorker* (Polity, 1990), p. 22.

28. Ibid., p. 248.

29. S. C. Neill, *Christian Faith Today* (Pelican, 1955), p. 174.

7. THE GREATEST OF ALL INVITATIONS

1. John Bunyan, *The Pilgrim's Progress*, Library of Classics (Collins, n.d.), pp. 47–48.

2. In Charles Wesley, *Hymns and Sacred Songs* (1742).

3. I can vouch for the truth of this anecdote, because I heard it from the lips of Professor James Stewart of New College, Edinburgh. I am surprised, therefore, that it is not included in *Life of the Late John Duncan*, written by David Brown and published in 1872 (Edmonston & Douglas, 2nd edn, revised). Nevertheless, David Brown did write of 'the child-like simplicity of the man' in prayer (p. 361).

4. Dietrich Bonhoeffer, *The Cost of Discipleship* (1937; English translation SCM, 1959), p. xxxiii.

5. Andrew Boyle, *Only the Wind will Listen: Reith of the BBC* (BBC, 1972), p. 18.

John Stott: A Timeline

April 27, 1921	Born in London
February 13, 1938	Conversion after hearing Eric (Bash) Nash preach
1938–1940	Decides to be ordained
October 1940	Enters Trinity College, Cambridge
June 1943	Graduates with double first
October 1944	Graduate studies in theology at Ridley Hall, Cambridge
December 21, 1945	Ordained deacon in St. Paul's Cathedral; becomes curate at All Souls
September 26, 1950	Instituted as rector of All Souls parish
January 1954	First book, *Men with a Message*, published
1954	Supports Billy Graham in Harringay Crusade
November 1955	Assistant missioner to Billy Graham at Cambridge
1956	Frances Whitehead appointed secretary
November 1956	Sails from Southampton for missions in the US and Canada
1958	*Basic Christianity* published. Missions in Australia
June 1959	Appointed chaplain to the Queen
Spring 1962	Second visit to Africa Visits to Keswick Convention begin
December 1964	First of six visits to Urbana Student Missions Convention, University of Illinois
October 18, 1966	Public disagreement with Dr Martyn Lloyd-Jones
April 1967	First National Evangelical Congress at Keele University
1968	Begins editing and contributing to The Bible Speaks Today series
December 1970	Speaks for third time at Urbana Student Missions Convention
April 1971	Begins to divert book royalties to Evangelical Literature Trust

Autumn 1972	Guest lecturer at Trinity Evangelical Divinity School, Deerfield, Illinois
January 1974	Scholars program begins, which will become Langham Partnership International
July 1974	Keynote address at Lausanne Congress; pleads for new balance between evangelism and social action; writes commentary on Lausanne Covenant he has drafted
1975	Becomes Rector Emeritus of All Souls; Michael Baughen becomes rector
November 1975	Adviser at fifth assembly of World Council of Churches First becomes known as 'Uncle John'
Summer 1977	Second visit to South America; visits Galapagos Islands
April to May 1980	In Eastern Europe
1981	Visits India and Bangladesh; meets Mother Teresa
January 1982	London Institute of Contemporary Christianity launched
1984	First edition of *Issues Facing Christians Today* published
1986	*The Cross of Christ* published
July 1989	Lausanne II, Manila, Philippines
August 1989	Sails up Amazon
1992	*The Contemporary Christian* published
1996	*The Message of 1 Timothy and Titus* published, the last of the seven volumes in the Bible Speaks Today series that he wrote himself
May 1998	Embolisms impair eyesight; gives up driving
January to February 1999	With study assistant John Yates to China, Thailand and Hong Kong
1999	*Evangelical Truth* launched at IFES World Assembly
January 31, 2000	With study assistant Corey Widmer in Kenya and Uganda; time with David Zac Niringiye

September 2001	Appoints Chris Wright as his successor as international director of Langham Partnership International
2003	*Why I Am a Christian* published
April 10, 2005	Listed by *Time* magazine as one of 100 most influential people in the world
2006	*Through the Bible, Through the Year* published
2007	*The Living Church* published
June 8, 2007	Moves to College of St. Barnabas, Lingfield, Surrey
July 17, 2007	Preaches at Keswick forty-five years after first visit
2010	*The Radical Disciple* published
July 27, 2011	Dies at the age of ninety